McGRAW-HILL

Netscape® 4
Communicator

Timothy J. O'Leary
Arizona State University

Linda I. O'Leary

Irwin
McGraw-Hill

Boston, Massachusetts   Burr Ridge, Illinois   Dubuque, Iowa
Madison, Wisconsin   New York, New York   San Francisco, California   St. Louis, Missouri

Irwin/McGraw-Hill

A Division of The McGraw·Hill Companies

Netscape® Communicator 4

Copyright © 1998 by The McGraw-Hill Companies, Inc. All rights reserved. Printed in the United States of America. Except as permitted under the United States Copyright Act of 1976, no part of this publication may be reproduced or distributed in any form or by any means, or stored in a data base or retrieval system, without the prior written permission of the publisher.

This book is printed on acid-free paper.

1 2 3 4 5 6 7 8 9 0 BAN BAN 3 2 1 0 9 8

ISBN 0-07-012579-1

The Sponsoring Editor was Rhonda Sands.
The Developmental Editor was Kristin Moore.
The Editorial Assistant was Stephen Fahringer.
The Production Supervisor was Richard DeVitto.
The cover was designed by Lorna Lo.
. Project management was by Elaine Brett, Fritz/Brett Associates.
Composition was by Pat Rogondino, Rogondino & Associates.
The typeface was ITC Clearface.
Banta Co. was the printer and binder.

Information has been obtained by The McGraw-Hill Companies, Inc. from sources believed to be reliable. However, because of the possibility of human or mechanical error by our sources, The McGraw-Hill Companies, Inc. or others, The McGraw-Hill Companies, Inc. does not guarantee the accuracy, adequacy, or completeness of any information and is not responsible for any errors or omissions or the results obtained from use of such information.

Library of Congress Cataloging Card Number 97-77855

http://www.mhhe.com

Contents

■ ■ ■ ■ ■ ■ ■ ■ ▪ ▫ ▫

Overview

The Internet and the World Wide Web

Every day you see references to the Internet in the newspaper, in TV ads, in popular soaps and sitcoms and more. You would need to be living in the backwoods not to hear or see references to such things as e-mail. What does all this mean to you? It means that in the future how you learn, do business, shop, or play will be different. Through the Internet you will find amusement, companionship, information—and tremendous opportunity. In the future, not knowing how to use the Internet would have an effect similar to not knowing how to read today.

Definition of Internet

What is the Internet? It is a network of thousands of computer networks that allows computers to communicate with each other. The popular term for the Internet is the "information highway." Like a highway, the Internet connects thousands of computers throughout the world, making available more information than you could read in a lifetime.

In 1993 the Internet connected 45,000 networks. Today's estimates are that between 2 and 4 million computers in 156 countries are connected to the Internet, and 25 to 35 million people have access to the Internet. In the United States alone 7 to 15 million people have access. The Internet is expected to continue growing from about 3.2 million computers today to over 100 million machines on all six continents. By 2000, it is estimated that there will be over one million networks connecting one billion users, with the majority of these users to be through at-home connections.

Things You Can Do on the Internet

The uses for the Internet are many and varied, and include the following:

- *Send and receive e-mail.* The largest use of the Internet is to send e-mail (electronic mail) messages between users. E-mail is the process that allows you to send and receive messages along Internet pathways to and from users at other computer sites.

- *Transfer files between computers.* File Transfer Protocol or FTP allows you to send (upload) or receive (download) files between computers. The files are made available on the hard drive of computers and are similar to an electronic library of information that can be accessed through the Internet by all users.

■ *Interact with other computers.* Telnet is software that gives users the ability to log on to another computer and run programs. It is a utility that lets you run other search or information services. Other "client software" is available if you have Windows or a Mac that does not use Telnet and connects you to a search service.

■ *Participate in discussion groups.* Newsgroups are databases of messages on a huge number of topics. Users participate in public discussions about the topic by sending e-mail messages to the newsgroup. Mailing lists are another type of discussion group consisting of a database of people interested in a particular topic. Your e-mail messages are mailed to the addresses of every participant in the mailing list. Chat groups, another type of discussion group, allow people to converse in real time.

■ *Search the World Wide Web.* The World Wide Web, also called the WWW or Web, allows users to quickly jump from one information source to another related source. These sources of information may be on the same computer or different computers around the world.

About the World Wide Web

The World Wide Web consists of information organized into pages containing text and graphic images. But most importantly, a page contains hypertext links, or highlighted keywords and images, that lead to related information. Clicking on the links quickly transports you to the location where that information is stored. The links may take you to other pages, text files, graphic images, movies, or audio clips. The Web allows users to view millions of pages of information by jumping from one related source to another by clicking on links.

To access the WWW, you must have a browser software program. Browsers display text and images, access FTP sites, and provide in one tool an uncomplicated interface to the Internet and WWW documents. Browsers allow you to surf the net unencumbered by the complexity of how to access information on the Internet. Two popular browser programs are Netscape's Communicator and Microsoft's Internet Explorer.

How Does Information Travel on the Internet?

The Internet uses a standard set of protocols, or rules for communication between computers. Protocols are a set of rules that establish guidelines for methods of communication to ensure uniformity among users. This allows various computer systems to connect and communicate.

TCP/IP (Transmission Control Protocol/Internet Protocol) is the core protocol used on the Internet. It breaks the information that is being transmitted into small packets of several hundred bytes each, including the addresses of sending and receiving computers. Each packet travels independently to its destination. The packets are sent along the network until they reach a router. Routers are the switchers of the system and are located at network intersections. Routers determine the best (fastest, most direct, least crowded) path for the packet to travel to reach its destination. There are many different paths to the same destination. As packets arrive at the destination, they are reassembled (they may arrive out of sequence). If a packet arrives damaged, it is requested to be sent again from the host. When reassembled, the source and destination address information are removed. The use of small packets helps the network to operate efficiently, so that load is distributed over the entire network, thereby avoiding overburdening any one part of the network.

Other protocols that are used are PPP and SLIP. PPP (Point to Point Protocol) creates an Internet connection that checks data transfer over lines and resends if damaged. SLIP (Serial Line Internet Protocol) is similar to PPP, but does not provide damage check.

How Do You Connect?

Many schools and businesses have direct access to the Internet using special high-speed communication lines and equipment. Students and employees are typically provided access through the organization's local area network (LAN) or through personal computers acting as dumb terminals (a terminal that attaches directly to a mainframe or other large computer).

Another way to access the Internet is through an Internet Service Provider (ISP) such as America Online and Microsoft Network. To access the ISP, you use your personal computer, modem, and telecommunications software to log onto the online service. Your computer is the client that links to a larger computer called the server, which runs special software that provides access to the Internet. You pay a fee for use of their service.

You may have free access to the Internet through a nearby city, college, or corporation. The level of access through these sources varies, as explained below.

- *Local Bulletin Board Systems (BBS).* Many BBSs have limited access to the Internet, commonly e-mail, mailing lists, and newsgroups, and do not offer nearly the amount of information as is available through the Internet. Also, many offer information on specialized topics only. You can find BBS telephone numbers through computer magazines and local computer newsletters.

- *Campus Computer Systems.* If you are affiliated with a college or university with an internal computer network that is connected to the Internet, you may be able to get "free" access (no charge directly to you—however, someone is paying). Access from outside the organization is generally via modem.

- *Corporate Network.* If you are affiliated with a corporation that is connected to the Internet, you may be able to get "free" access, generally via modem, similar to campus computer systems.

- *Libraries.* College and university libraries and many public libraries have replaced card catalogs with computer terminals tied to a central database. When colleges and universities connected to the Internet, the libraries were easily able to make their databases available. If they have the funds, public libraries may provide access to the Internet through their computer network.

■ *Freenets.* Freenets are community-based bulletin boards whose area of concern is community related. All have the same basic structure in that they are set up like an electronic town. The setup allows you to stop at different buildings to collect information about the community. Users must register to use the freenet. This is usually free to the community resident. Also, you can register as a guest, which allows you to look around and explore the freenet with limited access time. Freenets are directly accessible by modem (you need to locate the phone number). Some freenets also provide access to the Internet.

Netscape Communicator 4

Netscape Communicator 4.0 is a browser suite that comes in a Standard version and a Professional version. The Standard version includes the six components described below.

Component	Use
Navigator	Browse the WWW.
Messenger	Send and receive e-mail.
Collabra	Participate in discussion group messaging.
Composer	Create a Web page
Conference	Participate in real-time audio conferences and chat sessions, sketch on a shared whiteboard, and exchange and collaborate on files.
Netcaster	Automatically delivers selected information to your desktop and updates your Web sites.

The Professional version includes the additional components described below.

Component	Use
Calendar	A group scheduling program.
IBM Host On-Demand	Access central data on an IBM 3270 host.
AutoAdmin	Allows Communicator to be centrally managed, distributed, and updated.

Internet Terminology

Browser: A software program used to access and display WWW pages.

Download: To copy or receive a file from another computer using FTP.

E-mail: The process that allows you to send and receive messages along Internet pathways to and from users at other computer sites.

FTP: File Transfer Protocol allows you to upload or download files between computers.

Hypertext link: A connection to another Web page or to another location on the current page.

Internet: A network of thousands of computer networks that allows computers to communicate with each other.

ISP: An Internet service provider is a company that provides access to the Internet for a fee.

Mailing list: A discussion group in which e-mail messages are sent directly to the e-mail address of every participant in the mailing list.

Newsgroup: A discussion group in which e-mail messages are stored on centralized computer sites.

PPP: Point to Point Protocol creates an Internet connection that checks data transfer over lines and sends it again if damaged.

Protocol: A set of rules that establishes guidelines for methods of communication between computers to ensure uniformity among users.

Router: Switches on the Internet network system that are located at network intersections and determine the best path for the packet to travel to reach its destination.

SLIP: Serial Line Internet Protocol is similar to PPP, but does not provide damage check.

TCP/IP: Transmission Control Protocol/Internet Protocol is the core protocol used on the Internet.

Telnet: A software program that gives users the ability to log on to another computer and run programs.

Upload: To send a file to another computer using FTP.

WWW: The World Wide Web is a part of the Internet that consists of information organized into pages containing text and graphic images and hypertext links.

Case Study for Labs 1–5

As a recent college graduate, you have accepted your first job as a management trainee for The Sports Company. The Sports Company is a chain of discount sporting goods stores located in large metropolitan areas throughout the United States. The management trainee program emphasis is on computer applications in the area of retail management and requires that you work in several areas of the company.

In this series of labs, you are working in the marketing department. You have recently helped with setting up The Sports Company Web site. As part of your continued involvement in this project, you are using Netscape Communicator 4.0 to find information, send e-mail, and create a Web page.

Lab 1 The first WWW lab introduces you to Netscape Communicator's Navigator component. You will learn basic techniques for navigating the WWW and how to save and print pages.

Lab 2 This lab continues with the Navigator component and demonstrates how to use the search features to make finding information on the WWW much easier and more efficient.

Lab 3 In this lab you use the Messenger component of Netscape Communicator. You learn how to compose, send, reply to, forward, and delete e-mail messages. In addition, you learn how to create a personal address book.

Lab 4 This lab demonstrates the Collabra component, through which you learn how to find, read, and communicate with newsgroups. You will also learn how to subscribe and unsubscribe to a mailing list. In addition, you will learn how to use Yahoo's chat client to participate in online discussions.

Lab 5 In the last lab you use the Composer component to create a Web page.

Appendix Finally, the Appendix gives a short demonstration of three additional Internet tools: FTP, Telnet, and Gopher.

Before You Begin

To the Student:

The following resources are needed to complete these labs:

- Netscape Communicator 4 must be installed on your computer system. If the version of Netscape Communicator you are using is different from that used in this book, the menu selections and instructions in this manual may be slightly different.

- You need to have an Internet account with your school and an e-mail address.

- The data files required to complete this series of labs are provided by your instructor and should be copied to a new floppy disk.

- It is helpful if you are already familiar with how to use Windows-based applications.

In addition, you will learn while using the WWW that it is in a state of constant change. One day you can connect to a site and the next day you cannot. The information on a site may change from week to week. New sites are added and others are removed. There is no guarantee that the information you found one day will be there the next . . . however, you may just as easily find something new. Because things constantly change on the Internet, you need to be open to trying and searching. You may get lost, but you can always get home.

To the Instructor:

The following assumptions have been made:

- The version of Netscape on your computer system is Communicator 4.

- The Messenger component preferences are cleared when Netscape is exited. This allows the Mail and Discussion Group Setup Wizard to appear when Messenger is first accessed. If your setup is different and the wizard does not appear, students will need to set their preferences using Edit/ Preferences. Students will need e-mail addresses prior to setting Messenger preferences. Some systems allow the preferences to be saved for each student. If this is the case at your school, students will not need to re-enter their preferences each time they use Messenger.

- The default preferences are in effect each time Netscape is loaded.

- Accessing Telnet through Netscape requires that Netscape be appropriately configured.

Instructional Conventions

This text uses the following instructional conventions:

- Steps that you are to perform are preceded with a bullet (■) and are in blue type.

- Command sequences you are to issue appear following the word "Choose." Each menu command selection is separated by a /. If the menu command can be selected by typing a letter of the command, the letter will appear bold and underlined.

- Commands that can be initiated using a button and the mouse appear following the word "Click." The menu equivalent and keyboard shortcut appear in a margin note when the action is first introduced.

- Anything you are to type appears in bold text.

Navigating the Web

COMPETENCIES

After completing this lab, you will know how to:

1. Enter a URL.
2. Select links.
3. Use the history list.
4. Create and organize bookmarks.
5. View the HTML source code.
6. Save pages and images.
7. Use a form.
8. Print pages.

Case Study

The Sports Company has recently decided to take advantage of the Internet by creating a site on the WWW to market their products and advertise the company. In addition to the traditional commercial aspects of the site, such as a catalog of products, online order forms, and location information, they have included the first issue of *The Sports Company Update,* the monthly newsletter, to provide customers with health and fitness related information.

Your supervisor has asked you to look at the online newsletter and to make suggestions for improvements that would take better advantage of the Web.

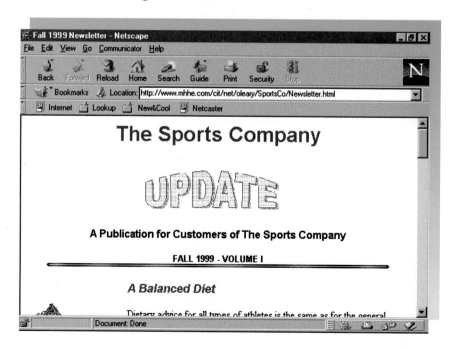

Concept Overview

The following concepts will be introduced in this lab:

1. Web Page
A Web page is a text file that has been created using a special programming language, called HyperText Markup Language, and that contains links to other Web pages and graphics.

2. Uniform Resource Locator
A Uniform Resource Locator (URL) provides location information that is used to navigate through the Internet to access a page.

3. Hypertext Link
A hypertext link, also called a hyperlink or simply a link, is a connection to another Web page or to another location on the current page.

4. Frame
Frames divide the Web browser's display into windows. Each window is a frame that can contain a separate, scrollable page.

5. Cache
A cache is a location in your computer system that stores the page information when it is downloaded from the network.

6. Bookmark
A bookmark permanently stores the URL of a page so that you can easily retrieve the page again.

7. HyperText Markup Language
All Web pages are written using a programming language called HyperText Markup Language (HTML).

8. Security
Security is low on transmissions of information over the Internet. To make transmissions secure, certificates, encryption, decryption, and digital signatures are used.

Exploring the Navigator Window

To view the newsletter on the WWW, you will use the **Navigator** component of the Netscape Communicator software application. Navigator is a **browser** program that is used to move to and display information located on the WWW.

■ If necessary, turn on your computer.

■ Double-click 🖼 Netscape Communicator.

If a Connect To dialog box appears, you will need to provide the required information to establish your Internet connection. This may require that you enter a user ID and password.

■ If necessary, enter the information needed by your school to establish your Internet connection.

■ Click Connect .

> If the Netscape shortcut is not on your desktop, choose Start/Programs/ Netscape/Netscape Navigator to load the program, or follow the directions provided by your school.

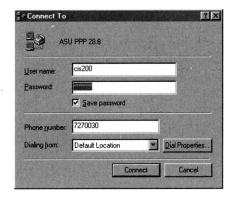

Your screen should be similar to Figure 1-1.

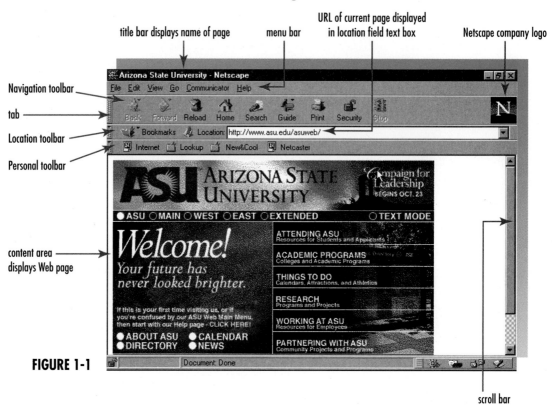

title bar displays name of page
menu bar
URL of current page displayed in location field text box
Netscape company logo

Navigation toolbar
tab
Location toolbar
Personal toolbar

content area displays Web page

FIGURE 1-1

scroll bar

If necessary, click 🔲 to maximize the window.

The Navigator component of Netscape Communicator launches by default on startup. The information displayed in the Navigator window on your screen will most likely be different from that shown in Figure 1-1. Your screen will probably display information about your school. This is because Netscape can be customized to display on startup different information than is specified in the program's setup procedure. In a few moments you will learn how to change the information displayed in Navigator so that it is the same as the figures in the text. Even though at present your screen displays different information, the components of the Navigator window are the same.

As in other Windows 95 applications, the Navigator window has a title bar, minimize 🔳 and maximize/restore 🔳 buttons, close button ❌, menu bar, toolbars, status bar, and scroll bars. The large center area of the window is the **content area** where the contents of a Web page are displayed.

Concept 1: Web Page

A **Web page** is a text file that has been created using a special programming language called HyperText Markup Language, and that contains links to other Web pages and graphics. The Web page is stored on a computer called a **server**, where it can be accessed and displayed using a browser program. A server may contain several Web sites. Each **Web site** consists of interconnected pages that have a common theme and design. Each Web page is designed by the people at the Web site and will contain information unique to that site.

Web pages are different from other types of text documents in two ways. First, they are interactive. This means the user can send information or commands to the Web site, which control a program running on the Web server, and receive a response from the site. Second, Web pages can use multimedia. This includes the ability to include animation on a page, display video, and run audio files.

When Navigator first loads, it displays the **startup home page**. This is a page that the Netscape program has been set to load by default. As mentioned earlier, most likely this is your school's home page. A **home page** is the first page of information for a Web site. Generally, home pages include a brief welcome with information about the site and a table of contents that will take you to other pages of information within the Web site.

You will learn more about HyperText Markup Language later in the lab.

The title bar displays the name of the page you are currently viewing. The six pull-down menus below the title bar when selected display Navigator commands that allow you to control the screen appearance and how Navigator performs, as well as provide Help information and general file utilities such as saving and printing. The general features in each menu are described below.

Menu	Use
File	Used to open, save, print, and perform other tasks related to files as well as perform tasks related to Communicator windows.
Edit	Used to cut, copy, paste, and search within the displayed window as well as to set preferences for customizing Communicator.
View	Controls the display of onscreen features such as toolbars, fonts, images, page content, and page information.
Go	Used to navigate among pages.
Communicator	Used to switch among Communicator components.
Help	Provides documentation and support services for using Communicator.

The toolbar buttons activate the most commonly used Navigator features. By default, the three toolbars, Navigation, Location, and Personal, are displayed when Navigator is first opened. Notice the ▯ bar to the left of each toolbar. This is called a **tab**. When you point to the tab, the name of the toolbar is displayed in a screen tip. In addition, dragging the tab allows you to change the order of the toolbars, and clicking it hides the toolbar to allow more space to display page content. When the toolbars are hidden, a single slim tab button is displayed for each hidden toolbar. Clicking the tab button redisplays the toolbar.

- Point to each toolbar's tab to identify it.
- Click on each toolbar's tab to hide all three toolbars.
- Redisplay the three toolbars.

hidden toolbars

> You can completely hide and then redisplay the toolbars and tabs using the Hide/Show commands on the View menu.

> You can also drag the toolbars to change their position.

The Navigation toolbar buttons, described below, are shortcuts for the most widely used commands, including those used to navigate among pages. To the right of the Navigation toolbar is the Netscape Company logo **N**. Clicking **N** will display Netscape's home page. It also animates whenever a page transfer is in progress.

> Pointing to a button displays a screen tip of information about that feature.

Button	Action
Back	Returns to previous page viewed.
Forward	Displays next page after using Back.
Reload	Accesses and redisplays page you are viewing.
Home	Displays home page.
Search	Displays a directory listing of Internet search engines.
Guide	Displays a menu containing links to Internet tools and information.
Print	Prints content of currently displayed page.
Security	Allows you to specify security related settings.
Stop	Interrupts transfer of incoming data.

The Location toolbar is used to access specific Web pages. It contains a Bookmarks button and a Location field text box. The Bookmarks button is used to store the location information to a page to make it easy to return to that page in the future. The Location field text box is used to enter the WWW address location of a page you want to display in the content area of the window. Currently the address for your home page is displayed. You will learn more about Web addresses shortly.

The Personal toolbar contains several buttons to help you locate information and can be customized to display buttons to your favorite locations on the Web. The default buttons included with Navigator are described below.

Button	Action
Internet	Displays a list of Internet search tools.
New&Cool	Used to find people and businesses on the Internet.
Lookup	Displays Netscape's list of selected new topics and popular topics.
Netcaster	Information delivery tool that must be subscribed to.

> Different default buttons may be displayed on the Personal toolbar, depending on the version of Netscape you are using.

The bar below the content area (shown below) contains a security indicator, progress bar, status message area, and Component bar. The security indicator on the left end of the bar indicates whether the transfer of information exchange you are engaged in is secure or not. When the transmission is not secure, the padlock icon appears as 🔓, and when it is secure, the padlock icon is locked 🔒. Most transfers of pages on the Web are not secure. This means the information can be read and intercepted by others, making the transfer of confidential information, such as credit card numbers, susceptible to abuse. Navigator includes features that allow you to make a transmission secure using a technology that makes the document an unreadable jumble during transit. This prevents an intermediary computer from accessing the document. Only the sending and receiving computers can read the document.

> Clicking the security icon will display a window containing information about the security features of the page you are viewing.

> You will learn more about Internet security later in this lab.

The progress bar illustrates the transfer's progress. If the amount of remaining time to load the page cannot be estimated, the bar bounces back and forth within its boundaries. The status message area reports on the progress of a transfer and displays information about the task you are performing.

The right end of this bar may display the Component bar consisting of four buttons that are used to access the four main component areas of Netscape Communicator. This bar can be displayed in two ways. Currently it is a **stationary palette** attached to the bottom right of the window. It can also appear as a **floating palette** in a separate small window that can be moved anywhere on the screen. Dragging the Component bar tab changes it to a floating palette, and clicking the 🗙 button in the floating palette window changes it to a stationary palette.

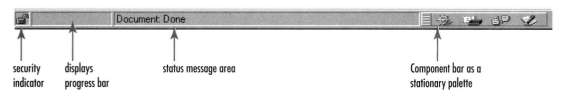

security indicator   displays progress bar   status message area   Component bar as a stationary palette

- If the component bar on your screen is a floating palette, change it to a stationary palette.

Component bar as floating palette

Entering a URL

Each Web page has its own address, called the Uniform Resource Locator (URL), which is displayed in the location field.

Concept 2: Uniform Resource Locator

A **Uniform Resource Locator (URL)** provides location information that is used to navigate through the Internet to access a page. Although URLs appear complicated, they are actually quite easy to decipher. The URL consists of several parts specifying the protocol, server, and path name of the item. Most begin with http://www or some variation. The URL for the Arizona State University home page is:

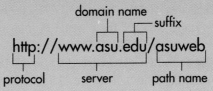

The protocol identifies the type of server where the information is stored. For WWW pages, the protocol is HTTP, for HyperText Transfer Protocol. Other protocols you will see are FTP (File Transfer Protocol), NEWS (Usenet), and GOPHER. A colon and two forward slashes (//) always follow the protocol. The server identifies the name of the computer system that stores the information. The server name typically begins with "WWW," indicating that the site is part of the World Wide Web. The second part is the domain name, which indicates the name of the institution that owns the site. The server name also includes a suffix that identifies the type of server. For example the suffix .com indicates the server is a commercial server, and .edu indicates it is an educational server. The last part is the path name, which indicates where the information is located on the server. Each part of the path is preceded with a single forward slash (/).

Refer to the Overview for a discussion of protocols.

A ~ (tilde) in a path name indicates a particular directory on the server.

There are several methods for browsing the WWW to view different pages of information. One is to enter the URL of the page you want to view in the Location field. Typing the URL will take you instantly to the location. You can find URLs for many WWW sites in books, news articles, on TV, and through discussion groups. When typing a URL, it must be entered exactly, including uppercase or lowercase. However, Netscape allows you to omit certain parts of the URL, because Navigator assumes these and automatically completes them for you. It is unnecessary to type:

- the protocol http://
- the www part of the server
- the suffix .com

If the URL protocol, path name, or suffix is different from those that are assumed, you must type them. Additionally, Navigator will attempt to complete the URL for you if there is a URL that was previously entered in the Location field that matches the letters you type. If you enter an incorrect URL, an error message will appear. The following table lists some common error messages and their meanings.

Message	Meaning
DNS Lookup Failed	DNS (domain name server) is a program that exists wherever you get your Internet access. It turns the Web site address that most users see (for example, www.aol.com) into a corresponding numerical address that can be read by a computer. A DNS Lookup Failed message indicates that the browser could not contact your domain name server, or that the domain name server was not aware of the site. Make sure the domain name is not misspelled.
File Not Found	The page may no longer exist, or it may have moved to another address.
Server Error or Server Busy Error	The computer you're trying to contact may be offline, may have crashed, or may be busy. You might want to try again later.

The Location field stores the last 14 URLs that were entered.

The first Web site you want to see is The Sports Company's home page. The URL for this page is http://www.mhhe.com/sportsco.

■ Click in the Location field.

■ Type **mhhe/sportsco**

■ Press (←Enter).

As the content of the page that the URL refers to is transferred or downloaded from the server location to your location, the Netscape company logo animates and the [Stop] button appears bright. Also, the status message area shows information such as the number of kilobytes loaded of the total number while the page loads, and the progress bar appears, visually showing the percentage completed. This information is important because many documents are very large and take a long time to load. When the page is fully downloaded, the message area indicates that the document transfer is complete, the progress bar is no longer active, and the [Stop] button may appear dimmed again.

You can also use **F**ile/**O**pen Page or (Ctrl) + O to display a location dialog box in which you enter the URL.

The current URL is highlighted and will be replaced by the new text as you type.

You can also click [▼] to the right of the Location field to display a menu of up to the last 14 URLs that have been entered in the Location field. Choosing a URL from the menu displays the page again.

Clicking [Stop] will cancel a transfer immediately.

Your screen should be similar to Figure 1-2.

FIGURE 1-2

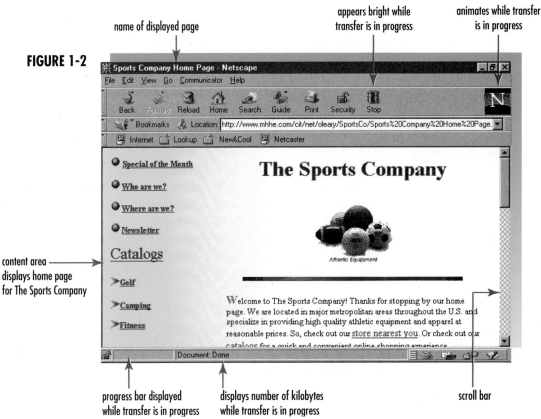

The content area displays the home page for The Sports Company, and the title bar displays the name of the current page. The Location field displays a different URL than you entered. This is because the URL you entered is a shortcut, called an **alias**, to the actual page address. A scroll bar appears whenever the content area is not large enough to fully display the entire page contents. To see the rest of the page,

■   Scroll the window to the bottom of the page.

Selecting Links

Probably the first thing you will notice about a page is the highlighted (under-lined or colored) text. This indicates a hypertext link.

Concept 3: Hypertext Link

A **hypertext link**, also called a **hyperlink** or simply a **link**, is a connection to another Web page or to another location on the current page. A link most commonly appears as colored and/or underlined text. Images or icons with colored borders may also be links. Clicking on a link displays the location or page associated with the requested link.

■ Point to the <u>Top</u> link.

Your screen should be similar to Figure 1-3.

FIGURE 1-3

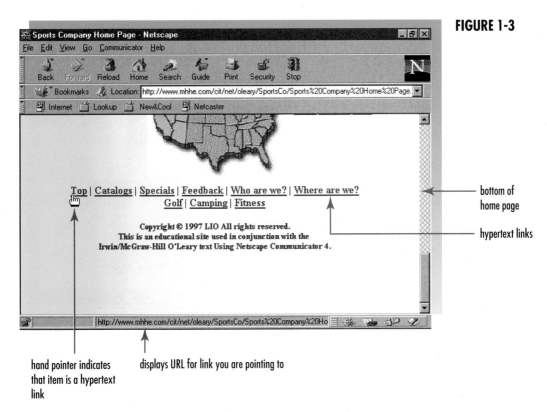

hand pointer indicates
that item is a hypertext
link

displays URL for link you are pointing to

bottom of
home page

hypertext links

Notice that the mouse pointer shape changed to a hand ⬢, indicating you are pointing to a hypertext link. In addition, the URL for this link appears in the status message area.

■ Click <u>Top</u>.

When you click this link, the top of the home page is displayed, saving you the trouble of scrolling back to the top of the page. This type of link is most often used when a Web page is a long document.

■ Click <u>Where are we?</u>

> Click a link only once and then watch the progress bar. Clicking again cancels the first operation and starts loading the page again. Be patient.

Your screen should be similar to Figure 1-4.

FIGURE 1-4

clicking the "Where
are we?" link displays
that section of the page

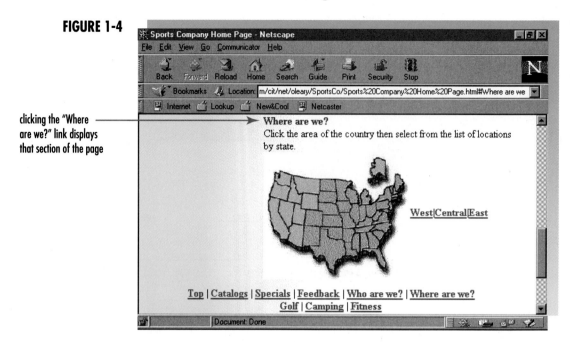

The section of the page appears that tells you how to find store locations is displayed. As you can see, this is much faster than scrolling.

Other links display a new page of information in the browser. When you click on a link, the location that the link refers to is transferred from the server location to your location. Watch the information in the status bar while the new page is loaded.

■   Click Top to return to the top of the page.

■   Click Special of the Month.

Your screen should be similar to Figure 1-5.

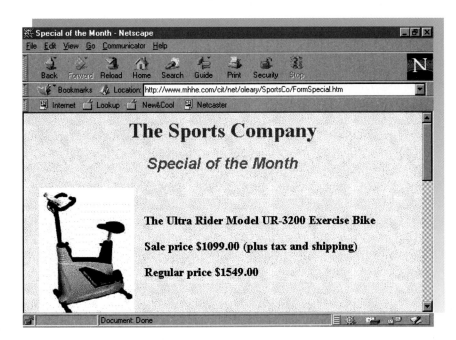

FIGURE 1-5

The title bar displays the title of the current page and the Location field shows the new URL for this page. Next you want to see the Catalogs page.

■ Scroll to bottom of the page.

You have probably noticed that the links on this page are in different colors. The default colors for links are blue and purple. A link that appears in blue indicates it has not been selected recently. This is called an **unfollowed link**. A purple link indicates that the link has been recently used, and is thus called a **followed link**. It will remain a followed link for a set period of time, depending upon your program setup (the default is 30 days).

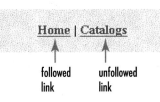

followed link   unfollowed link

Many of the links on The Sports Company site may appear as followed links if a previous user on your computer recently selected them.

■ Click Catalogs.

Your screen should be similar to Figure 1-6.

FIGURE 1-6

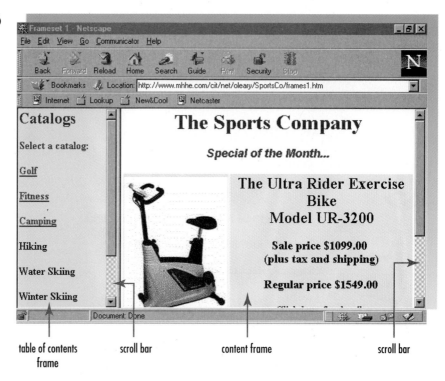

table of contents frame   scroll bar   content frame   scroll bar

The content area is divided into two windows called frames.

Concept 4: Frame

You can adjust the size of the frames by dragging the border between frames.

Frames divide the Web browser's display into windows. Each window is a frame that can contain a separate, scrollable page. A group of frames is called a **frame set**. A frame set is a special Web page that defines the size and location of each window. Clicking on a frame makes it the active frame, and its URL appears in the Location field. When a frame is active, many of the toolbar and menu commands affect only the active frame. The left frame is commonly used as a table of contents to other areas in the frame set. The right frame called the **content frame**, displays the contents of the selected page.

Frames are used when you want the contents of one part of the Web browser's display to remain unchanged while the contents of other parts change based on hyperlinks that the user selects.

- Scroll the table of contents frame.

- Click Camping.

- As the page loads, scroll the content frame.

Your screen should be similar to Figure 1-7.

FIGURE 1-7

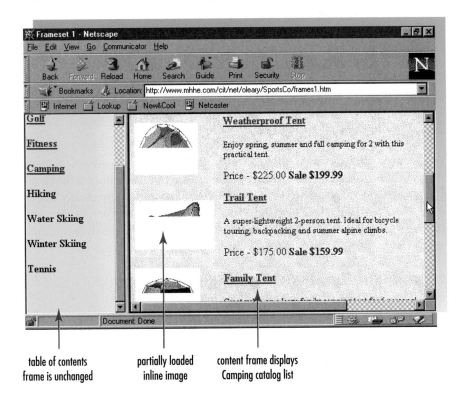

table of contents
frame is unchanged

partially loaded
inline image

content frame displays
Camping catalog list

Information related to the topic you selected appears in the content frame. The frame on the left does not change, allowing you to quickly select a different category. Navigator loads the text of a page first, followed by images. Images first appear as empty boxes containing a small image icon 🖻. As the image is loaded it replaces the box.

You probably noticed that this page took slightly longer to load. This is because it contains many pictures. Picture images are much larger in byte size than text and therefore take considerably longer to load. Usually when people design pages, they take this factor into consideration, making the images small so the page loads faster. Images that are part of a page are called **inline images**, because they load automatically as part of the page. Because Navigator loads text first and then graphics, you can read the text while the graphics continue to load.

Because the images are small, this helps the page load faster, but it is difficult to see the items well. Many times an image will be a link to a page that displays the picture full size. This is called a **thumbnail** image.

■ Click on the first tent thumbnail to see it full size.

■ Click 🔙.

> You can turn off loading of inline images to speed up loading of pages by using **E**dit/Pr**e**ferences/Advanced and clearing the Automatically Load **I**mages checkbox. Then, if you want to see the graphics on a particular page, you can click 🖼 to load the graphics for that page only.

> The menu equivalent is **G**o/**B**ack, and the keyboard shortcut is Alt + ←.

The menu equivalent is <u>G</u>o/<u>F</u>orward, and the keyboard shortcut is ⟨Alt⟩ + ⟨→⟩.

Pointing to [Back] and [Forward] displays a screen tip with the title of the page that will be displayed.

The previously viewed page is displayed again. Likewise, clicking [Forward] will display the next page you viewed. [Forward] is only available after using [Back].

To see more information about the First-Aid Kit,

■   Click <u>First-Aid Kit</u>.

This page provides detailed information about the item and a button to access the order page.

Using the History List

You have selected several links that have taken you to different pages of information. While you are using Navigator, the program maintains a history of the places you have visited, called a **history list**. Rather than returning to a previously viewed page one at a time using the [Back] button, you can select a page you have viewed from the history list. To see the history list,

■   Choose <u>G</u>o.

The bottom section of the Go menu displays a list of the page titles you have viewed since loading Netscape. The most recently viewed page is at the top of the list. It will not display a complete list of items if you have returned to a previously viewed page, because it clears the list to display only the most recent series of pages. Clicking on any one of these will quickly return you to that location. As you make more selections, the older selections are removed from the history list. To return to the home page,

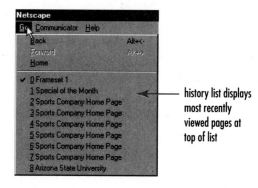

history list displays most recently viewed pages at top of list

■   Click Sports Company Home Page.

■   If necessary, move to the top of the page.

The home page for The Sports Company is reloaded and displayed in the content area. The page is not downloaded again from the server, instead it is reloaded from a file that was created and stored temporarily in a cache folder on your computer.

Concept 5: Cache

A **cache** is a location in your computer system that stores the page information when it is downloaded from the network. There are two types of caches, a memory cache and a disk cache. Memory cache is temporary and clears when you end your Netscape session, whereas disk cache stores the page information in a folder on your hard disk that does not clear when you end your session. When the space allocated for disk cache is full, old files are cleared automatically to make space for the new information.

Normally, the first time you request a page, Navigator retrieves the page from the network and stores the page information in both caches. If you request a page you have seen before during your current session, Navigator first checks to see if the page is available in cache. If it is available, it loads the page from cache rather than the network because it is much faster and reduces network traffic.

In some cases, you might not want a page to be retrieved from cache. For example, many news service pages update the page information throughout the day, making the page you displayed initially different from the page currently offered by the network. If a modification to a particular URL has occurred, you may want the updated page rather than the old copy stored in a cache. If you click a link, choose a bookmark, type a URL, or click the [Reload] button, Navigator checks with the server to see if an update has occurred before bringing a page from cache. If any change to the page has occurred, a fresh version is downloaded; otherwise, a copy is quickly retrieved from cache.

If you click the [Reload] button while holding down the [⇧Shift] key, Navigator downloads a fresh version from the network regardless of whether the page has been updated. Cache is not used. This type of reload is useful if you suspect the cached copy of a page has been corrupted.

When you click the [Back] button or choose a history item, Navigator does not check the network. Since you are explicitly requesting a previously viewed page, Navigator tries first to retrieve the cached copy (if still present in the cache) even if the server offers a more recent version.

You can customize cache settings using the Cache preferences panel. To display this panel, choose **E**dit/Pr**e**ferences/Advanced and select Cache. You can change the preferences to check cache once per session, every time, and never. The default setting is once per session.

> The menu equivalent is **V**iew/**R**eload, and the keyboard shortcut is [Ctrl] + R.

> You will learn about bookmarks shortly.

A more complete history list is also maintained by Navigator. To see this listing,

- Choose **C**ommunicator/**H**istory.

> The keyboard shortcut is [Ctrl] + H.

The History window on your screen should be similar to Figure 1-8.

FIGURE 1-8

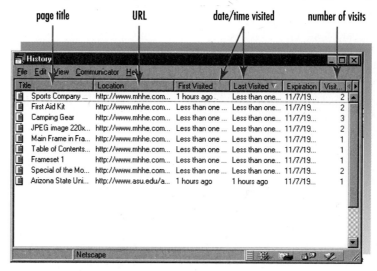

The History window displays page titles that have been recently viewed. The number of days that this history list is stored is determined by the length of time set in the Navigator program. When the specified number of days is reached, the pages are cleared from the list. As you can see, this window includes much more information on each page than the Go menu. In addition to the page's title, it includes the URL, when the page was first and last visited, the expiration date, and number of visits. It also includes a menu containing many of the same features as the Navigator menu bar.

Figure 1-8 displays a history list of pages from the current session only. Yours will probably display many pages from a longer time period.

■   Click ☒ to close the History window.

Creating and Organizing Bookmarks

If you wanted to return to The Sports Company home page in a future session, you would need to retype the URL in the Location field. When you find places that you would like to return to later, you can mark the location by creating a bookmark.

> **Concept 6: Bookmark**
>
> A **bookmark** permanently stores the URL of a page so that you can easily retrieve the page again. The bookmarks are stored in a list that is saved on the hard disk. Each item in the list contains the title of the page, the associated URL and some additional date information. The bookmark remains on the list until you delete it.

You will create a bookmark for The Sports Company home page you are currently viewing.

The menu equivalent is **C**ommunicator/ **B**ookmarks.

■   Click 🔖 Bookmarks .

The Bookmarks pop-up menu displays the three bookmark menu options at the top of the menu and the list of bookmark folders and saved bookmarks on your computer. Navigator includes a preset group of bookmarks with the program that are divided into folders to help better organize the list. Each folder is preceded with the 📁 icon. Each bookmark item displays the title of the page and is preceded with the 📑 icon.

■ Point to the Entertainment bookmark folder.

A submenu displays the list of bookmark items included in this category.

> America Online
> The Dilbert Zone
> Disney
> GameCenter
> Internet Movie Database
> The Internet Underground Music Archive
> Match.Com
> TV Guide
> Warner Bros. Online

To create a bookmark for the currently displayed page,

■ Choose Add Bookmark.

Next you will return to your startup home page and then try using the bookmark.

■ Click 🏠 Home .

■ Click 🔖 Bookmarks .

The Bookmark menu displays the page title of the page you bookmarked at the bottom of the bookmark list.

■ Click the Sports Company Home Page bookmark.

The bookmarked page contents are reloaded. You will find creating and using bookmarks to be a very handy timesaver.

Next, you want to change the location of the bookmark.

■ Click 🔖 Bookmarks .

As you add more bookmarks to your list, it is convenient to add related bookmarks to folders you create or to an appropriate pre-existing folder. You decide to move this bookmark to the Shopping folder.

■ Choose Edit Bookmarks.

> If the Entertainment bookmark folder is not listed, point to any available folder.

> You can also drag the Page Proxy icon 📄 located to the left of the Location text box to the Bookmark button to add a bookmark for the current page.

> The menu equivalent is **G**o/**H**ome.

> Using the File Bookmark menu option, you can specify a bookmark folder to add the bookmark to.

Your screen should be similar to Figure 1-9.

FIGURE 1-9

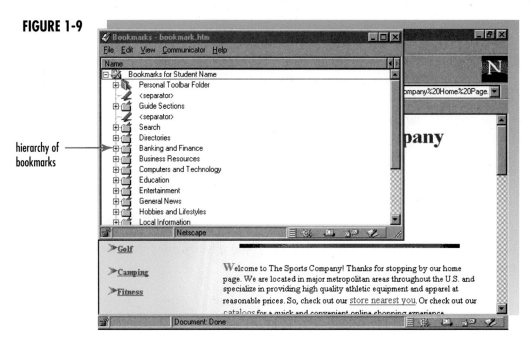

hierarchy of bookmarks

The Bookmarks window is open and displays the entire bookmark list as a hierarchy. This is similar to how folders and files on your hard disk are displayed in Window's Explorer. The menu options help you organize your list by allowing you to add and delete folders and bookmarks. Additionally, you can use drag and drop to rearrange your bookmarks. To move The Sports Company bookmark item to the Shopping folder,

> If a Shopping folder is not listed, use **F**ile/New **F**older to create a new bookmark folder named Shopping.

> The bookmark folder will appear highlighted when it is the selected folder to receive the bookmark.

> As you drag, a horizontal line shows you where the bookmark will be placed when you release the mouse button.

> Clicking ⊟ hides all bookmarks in the folder.

> The menu equivalent is **F**ile/**C**lose and the keyboard shortcut is Ctrl + W.

> From the Bookmarks window, you double-click a bookmark to go to it.

> You can also create an Internet shortcut on your desktop by dragging a link from a page directly to the desktop. Double-clicking the desktop icon will open the browser and load the particular page.

- Select the Sports Company Home Page bookmark icon and drag it to the Shopping folder.

- If necessary, click the [icon] to the left of the Shopping folder to display the list of bookmarks in the folder.

- Drag the Sports Company Home Page bookmark icon to the correct alphabetical location within the folder.

- Click ☒ to close the Bookmarks window.

You can also create a bookmark from the Navigator window by pointing to a link and dragging it to the  button or into an open Bookmarks window.

- Drag the Catalogs link to the [Bookmarks] button and then to the correct alphabetical location in the Shopping folder.

- Click [Bookmarks] and choose the Catalogs bookmark in the Shopping folder.

The Catalogs page is reloaded and displayed.

Because you may be using different computers at school, you can save your personal bookmark list to a file on your floppy disk. To do this,

■ Insert a floppy disk into the appropriate drive.

■ Click [Bookmarks] and choose Edit Bookmarks.

■ Choose File/Save As.

The keyboard shortcut is Ctrl + S.

From the Save Bookmarks File dialog box, you need to specify a file name for the bookmark, and the location.

■ Change the file name to My Bookmarks and specify the drive containing your data disk as the location.

■ Click [Save].

The entire bookmark list is saved to the disk. The next time you are using another computer, you can access your bookmark list from the disk using the File/Import command in the Bookmark window. The bookmarks are added to the beginning of the existing bookmark file list.

Bookmark files are saved as HTML file format.

You will find as time goes by that you have an extensive list of bookmarks, many of which you no longer need. To keep your list up to date, you can quickly delete them.

■ Select the two bookmarks you added to the Shopping category.

■ Press Delete.

■ Close the Bookmarks window.

Hold down Ctrl while clicking the bookmark icons to select them both.

The menu equivalent is Edit/Delete.

As a courtesy to others, delete any bookmarks you add to a shared computer.

Viewing the HTML Source Code

Next you want to return to The Sports Company's home page and look at the newsletter.

■ Redisplay The Sports Company home page.

■ Click Newsletter.

Your screen should be similar to Figure 1-10.

FIGURE 1-10

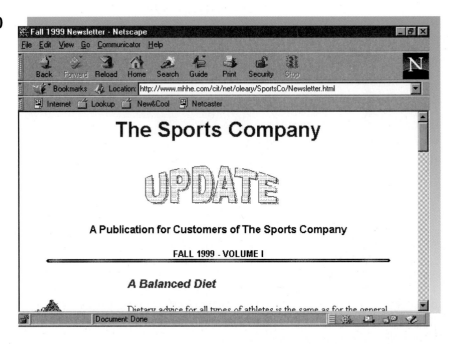

You are very pleased with how the online version of the newsletter looks. It is not in exactly the same style layout as the printed version because it had to be converted to a HyperText Markup Language (HTML) document.

Concept 7: HyperText Markup Language

You will learn more about HTML in Lab 5.

All Web pages are written using a programming language called **HyperText Markup Language (HTML)**. HTML commands control how the information on a page is displayed, such as font colors and size, and how an item will be processed, such as a form. HTML also allows users to click on highlighted text or images and jump to other locations on the same page, other pages in the same site, or to other sites and locations on the Web altogether. HTML commands are interpreted by the browser software program you are using to access the WWW.

To display the HTML commands or source code for the page you are viewing,

The keyboard shortcut is Ctrl + U.

■   Choose View/Page Source.

Your screen should be similar to Figure 1-11.

FIGURE 1-11

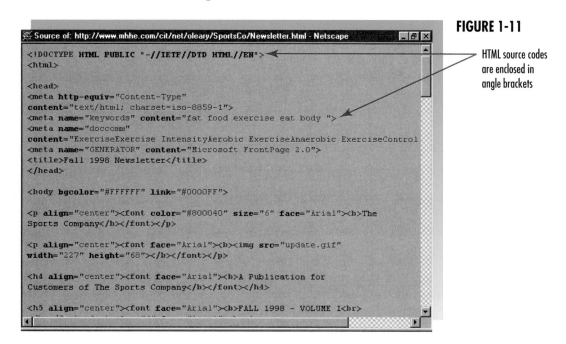

HTML source codes
are enclosed in
angle brackets

A second window is opened to display the document source code. The source code consists of instructions enclosed in angle brackets (<>) that identify the different parts of the page and control how the text is displayed.

■   Click ☒ to close the Source window.

■   Scroll the newsletter to quickly skim the topics.

Saving Web Pages and Images

The articles in this newsletter are general in nature. The first article discusses the basics of a healthy diet and the second the benefits of exercise. You decide you want to save a copy of the newsletter so you can read and refer to it later as you prepare your suggestions on how to improve the online newsletter.

When you click on a link to a page, sound, or video link, the file is downloaded and temporarily stored on your computer system. Navigator automatically displays the file if it is a text or HTML document, or if possible runs the appropriate software program to "play" the file to view or hear it.

Saving a page you are viewing saves a copy of the downloaded file to your disk. Saving a link copies the file referenced in the link to your disk by downloading it but not displaying it. Often you may want to save page content to disk rather than read it online. This saves both online time (important when you are paying for time with a service provider) and paper. To save the current page to your data disk,

The keyboard shortcut is ⌈Ctrl⌉ + S.

The **F**ile/Save **F**rame As command saves the current frame to disk.

■   Choose **F**ile/**S**ave As.

The Save As dialog box is displayed. You can save the page as a plain text file (.txt) or an HTML file. A plain text file does not retain any of the original page's formatting. You can open and modify a text file with any word processor. You can also view, but not modify, a text file using Navigator's File/Open command. Saving the page in HTML file format saves all the formatting of the original page, which then can be viewed using the browser (offline).

■   Specify the drive containing your data disk as the location.

■   Change the file type to Plain Text [*.txt].

If you do not want to display the page to save, you can point to the link and choose **S**ave Link As from the shortcut menu.

■   Delete the HTML file extension from the file name.

■   Click [**Save**].

Do not use a /, :, or # symbol in file names.

The file is saved to your data disk and can be viewed using any word processor program. It will not include the formatting or images. You can also save just the images from pages. Images are commonly saved as .gif or .jpg file types that can be opened and viewed using graphics programs such as Paint or a browser. You could also use any Windows word processor to view images of this type. You decide to save the image of the food guide pyramid to your data disk.

■   Right-click the image of the food guide pyramid.

■   From the shortcut menu, choose Save Image As.

■   If necessary, specify your data disk as the location to save the file.

■   Click [**Save**].

You can also highlight and copy selected page content to the Clipboard and then paste it into any word processor file. When copying and saving information from a Web page, be aware of the copyright protection associated with the page. This information is usually displayed at the bottom of the page. You may need the author's permission if you plan to use the information commercially, otherwise cite appropriately by giving credit as in a footnote of a research paper.

■   Return to The Sports Company home page.

Using Forms

The last feature you want to check out is the feedback form. Notice the animated image of an envelope along the left side of the page. Clicking the image will open a **form** in which you complete and then submit your information.

You may need to scroll the page to see the Feedback mail icon.

■   Click the Feedback mail icon.

Your screen should be similar to Figure 1-12.

FIGURE 1-12

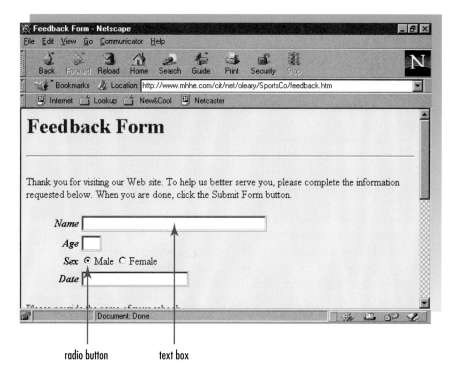

radio button   text box

Forms typically include fields in which you type information, checkboxes, radio buttons, pop-up menus, selection lists, and buttons for sending and clearing the information you enter. Once you complete the form, you click the button to send the form's content to the recipient. It is not necessary to address the form, as it is automatically included in the form design.

> A form's content is sent to the recipient using e-mail. You will learn about e-mail in Lab 3.

- ■ Complete the requested information in the form.

- ■ Click [Submit Form].

Netscape displays a Security Information dialog box warning you that
the information you are sending is
not secure. This means it could be
intercepted and used by an unin-
tended recipient.

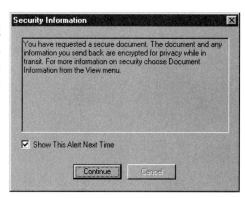

Concept 8: Security

Security is low on transmissions of information over the Internet. This is because as your message travels to the recipient, it is temporarily stored on many computers en route, making your message available to be read by others. The three most common types of security invasions are **eavesdropping**, in which a third party listens in on a private conversation, **manipulation**, in which the message is intercepted and changed, and **impersonation**, where a sender or receiver uses a false identity for communication.

As the Internet has developed it is being used more and more for commercial purposes, so that security considerations have become extremely important. To reassure customers that the information they submit, such as credit card numbers and address information, is safe, browser software programs have made available to Web servers sophisticated methods to secure transmissions. These include the use of certificates, encryption, decryption, and digital signatures.

A **certificate** is a tamper-resistant file that identifies the individual to whom it is issued. It is issued by a certificate signer, a company that verifies and authorizes certificate requests. The certificate includes the tools, called public and private keys, needed to create a secure communication. A **public key** is the **encryption** code that is used to scramble the information in an outgoing message so that no one else can read it. A **private key** is a **decryption** code that is used to unscramble the message that was encrypted with the public key. The private key can only be used to decrypt messages that were created using the public key. The public key can be sent to anyone you want and is included with your digital signature. The recipient stores your public key and can use it to encrypt and send information to you.

A **digital signature** when added to a message assures that the message was actually sent by the sender, not from an impersonator. The signature is checked by the recipient's software. Because anyone can send an encrypted message using another person's public key, they can just as easily say they are the sender. But only the sender can digitally sign a message that can be verified by anyone who has their public key.

The security indicator will tell you whether or not a message is secure. Further information about a message's security can be obtained by clicking [Security] or choosing **C**ommunicator/**S**ecurity Info.

Currently, certificates are issued to organizations running servers and are not issued to Netscape Navigator users. Without a certificate, the server can only operate insecurely.

A URL that begins with https: (instead of http:) indicates that a page comes from a server with encryption features.

■ Click [Continue].

Your screen should be similar to Figure 1-13.

FIGURE 1-13

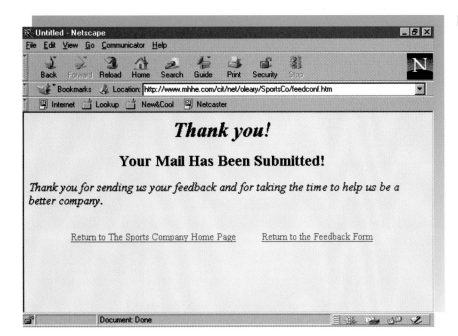

A confirmation message is displayed indicating the feedback form was received.

Printing Web Pages

It is also convenient to simply print the content of the current page. For example, if you have completed a form to order an item, you may want to have a printed copy as your confirmation of your order. Before printing, however, it is a good idea to preview the page first to see how it will look and to avoid wasting paper.

■ Click [Back] to display the completed Feedback Form page again.

■ Choose File/Print Preview.

Your screen should be similar to Figure 1-14.

FIGURE 1-14

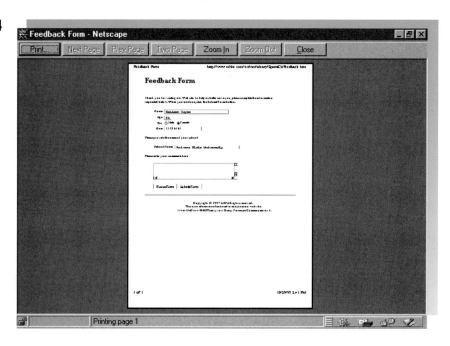

Navigator reformats the page content to fit the paper size by repositioning the text and graphics as needed. Printing a page prints the images as well as all the text formatting. Finally, to print the page,

■   Click Print... .

The Print dialog box on your screen should be similar to Figure 1-15.

> To increase and decrease the magnification of the page, use the Zoom In and Zoom Out buttons or simply click on the preview image.

> If the page content is longer than a single printed page, use the Next Page and Prev Page buttons to view additional pages.

> The menu equivalent is **F**ile/**P**rint.

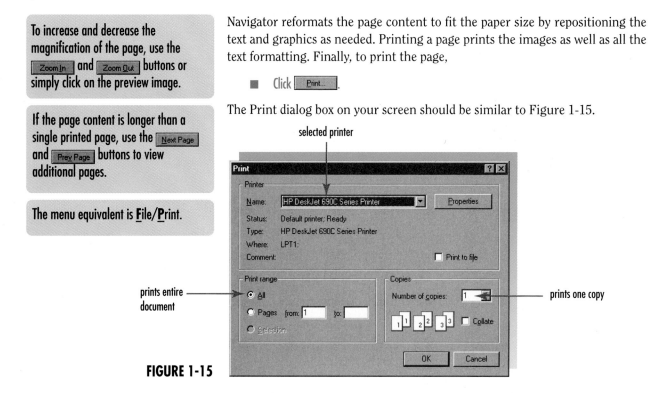

selected printer

prints entire document

prints one copy

FIGURE 1-15

■ Select the appropriate printer for your system from the Printer Name drop-down list box.

■ Click [OK].

To exit the Netscape Communicator program,

■ Click ⊠.

■ If necessary, disconnect from the Internet.

> If a page is divided into frames, the File menu option changes to Print Frame. The currently selected frame is printed.

> The [Print] toolbar button will display the Print dialog box.

> The menu equivalent is File/Exit or Ctrl + Q.

LAB REVIEW

■ ■ ■ ■ ■ ■ ■ ■ ■ ■ ■ ■

Key Terms

alias   (NET16)
bookmark   (NET24)
browser   (NET9)
cache   (NET23)
certificate   (NET32)
content area   (NET10)
content frame   (NET20)
decryption   (NET32)
digital signature   (NET32)
eavesdrop   (NET32)
encryption   (NET32)
floating palette   (NET13)
followed link   (NET19)
form   (NET30)
frame   (NET20)
frame set   (NET20)
history list   (NET22)
home page   (NET11)
hyperlink   (NET16)
hypertext link   (NET16)
HyperText Markup Language (HTML)   (NET28)
impersonation   (NET32)
inline image   (NET21)

link   (NET16)
manipulation   (NET32)
Navigator   (NET9)
private key   (NET32)
public key   (NET32)
server   (NET11)
startup home page   (NET11)
stationary palette   (NET13)
tab   (NET12)
thumbnail   (NET21)
unfollowed link   (NET19)
Uniform Resource Locator (URL)   (NET14)
Web page   (NET11)
Web site   (NET11)

Command Summary

Command	Shortcut Key	Button	Action
File/Open Page	Ctrl + O		Opens a page from disk
File/Save As	Ctrl + S		Saves current document to disk
File/Save Frame As			Saves current frame to disk
File/Print Preview			Displays document onscreen as it will appear when printed
File/Print		Print	Prints current document
File/Print Frame			Prints current frame
File/Close	Ctrl + W		Closes current window
File/Exit	Ctrl + Q	☒	Exits Netscape
Edit/Preferences/Advanced/ Automatically load images			Turns on and off display of inline image
View/Page Source	Ctrl + U		Displays HTML code for current page
View/Hide/Show Navigation Toolbar			Hides or displays Navigator toolbar
View/Hide/Show Location Toolbar			Hides or displays Location toolbar
View/Hide/Show Personal Toolbar			Hides or displays Personal toolbar
View/Reload	Ctrl + R	Reload	Reloads current page
Go			Displays list of pages viewed since loading Netscape
Go/Back	Alt + ←	Back	Displays last viewed page
Go/Forward	Alt + →	Forward	Displays next viewed page after using Back
Go/Home		Home	Displays startup home page
Communicator/Bookmarks/ Add Bookmark	Ctrl + D		Saves URL of current page
Communicator/Bookmarks/ Edit Bookmarks	Ctrl + B		Modifies location of stored bookmark
Communicator/History	Ctrl + H		Displays detailed history of pages viewed in History window
Communicator/Security Info		Security	Displays information about a page's security settings

Bookmarks Window:

Command	Shortcut Key	Button	Action
File/New Folder			Creates a new bookmark folder
File/Go to bookmark			Redisplays saved page
File/Close	Ctrl + W		Closes Bookmarks window
Edit/Delete	Delete		Removes bookmark from list

Fill-In Questions

1. Complete the following statements by filling in the blanks with the correct terms.

a. A text file that contains links to other Web pages and graphics is called a _____.

b. The _____ is the first page of information for a Web site.

c. The _____ is the address for the Web page.

d. When the Component bar is not attached at the bottom right part of the window, it appears as a _____.

e. A connection to another Web page or another location on the current page is indicated by a _____.

f. _____ images are part of a page, because they load automatically as part of the page.

g. _____ divide the Web browser's display into separate windows.

h. A _____ temporarily saves page information on your computer.

i. A _____ permanently stores the URL so that you can return to it at any time.

j. The _____ programming language controls how information is displayed on a Web page.

2. In the following Navigator screen, letters identify important elements. Enter the correct term for each screen element in the space provided.

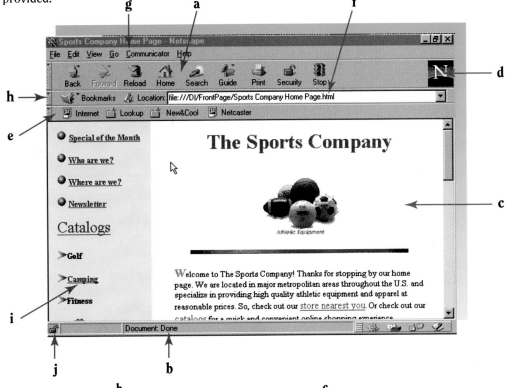

a. _____   b. _____   c. _____

d. _____   e. _____   f. _____

g. _____   h. _____   i. _____

j. _____

Matching

1.

2. HTML

3. home page

4. encryption

5.

6.

7. Navigator

8. URL

9. hypertext link

10. bookmark

_____ **a.** displays the startup home page

_____ **b.** Communicator component used to browse the WWW

_____ **c.** a connection to another Web page or location on the current page

_____ **d.** programming language used to create Web pages

_____ **e.** terminates transmission of a page

_____ **f.** the scrambling of outgoing information

_____ **g.** WWW address

_____ **h.** retrieves page again from server

_____ **i.** saved link to Web page

_____ **j.** opening page of a Web site

Discussion Questions

1. What is a hypertext document?
2. Explain how a message can be made secure.
3. How are the hypertext links identified in Navigator?

4. What is a URL? Explain the parts of a URL.
5. Explain history lists and bookmarks.

Hands-On Practice Exercises

■ ■ ■ ■ ■ ■ ■ ■ ■ ■ ■

Step by Step

Rating System

☆ Easy
☆☆ Moderate
☆☆☆ Difficult

☆

1. In this problem you will learn about the Netscape Communicator's Help system. Netscape has a detailed Help system similar to Help systems in other Windows applications.

  a. Choose Help/Help Contents from the Navigator menu. The Help system is divided into three areas: Contents, Index, and Find. Contents is the area that is selected by default. Selecting a topic from the Contents list in the left frame displays the topic description in the right frame.

  b. Read the overview about Navigator, then click the link <u>Using Navigator</u>. Locate information about viewing bookmarks. What are the five steps to add a bookmark folder?

  c. Choose Find. In the Find What text box, type: About the Internet. Read the information located on this topic. What do the client and server computers do?

☆

2. In this problem you will continue to explore The Sports Company's Web site.

  a. Start Netscape Communicator.

  b. Enter the URL http://www.mhhe.com/sportsco in the Location field.

c. Click the <u>Where are we?</u> link. What is the address of the store in Tempe, AZ?

d. Display the Golf Gear catalog page. Follow the Golf Bag link and display the image full size.

e. Save the Golf Bag page to your data disk as a plain text file. Save the golf bag image to your data disk.

f. You decide to order the aerobic stepper. Locate this item and complete steps 1 and 3 of the order form. Preview and print the completed order form.

g. Return to the site's home page.

h. Exit Communicator.

i. Open the text file of the Golf Bag page you saved to your data disk using any word processor program. Add your name and the current date to the top of the file and print it.

j. Open the text file of the newsletter you saved to your data disk during the lab using any word processor program. Add your name and the current date to the top of the file. Print the file.

k. Using a graphics program such as Paint, open the image file of the food guide pyramid that you saved during the lab or insert it into a word processor file. Then print the image. In the same manner, print the image of the Golf Bag file you saved.

l. Exit all programs, saving any changes you made to the files.

3. In this problem you will practice navigating the WWW by exploring your school's Web site.

a. Start Netscape Communicator. If your startup home page is not your school's Web site, enter the URL of your school's home page.

b. Select links on your school Web site. Try to locate some of the following information. *Note:* If your school does not have a site set up, use the site at Arizona State University (www.asu.edu/asuweb).

- Department you are majoring in
- On-campus activities
- Sporting events
- Class instructor

- Admissions
- Calendar of events

c. Save one of the pages to your data disk as a plain text file.

d. Preview and print another page.

e. Return to the site's home page.

f. Exit Communicator.

g. Open the text file of the page you saved to your data disk using any word processor program. Add your name and the current date to the top of the file and print it.

h. Exit the word processor program, saving changes you made to the file.

4. One of the most popular comic strips is Dilbert. Like many other comic strips, Dilbert has its own Web site.

a. Start Netscape Communicator.

b. Enter the address http://www.unitedmedia.com/comics/dilbert/.

c. Explore the site and find the answers to the following questions.

- What are the names of the two main characters?
- Who is the creator of Dilbert?
- What is Dogbert's ruling class? (See DNRC.)

d. Read the most recent newsletter.

e. Print the most recent Sunday strip.

f. Return to the site's home page.

g. Exit Communicator.

5. You are planning a trip to the Grand Canyon and want to find out information about the park.

a. Start Netscape Communicator.

b. Enter the address http://www.kaibab.org/.

c. Go on a virtual visit of the Grand Canyon. When you finish, return to the home page.

d. Select the appropriate screen resolution for your system with frames to view this site.

e. Explore the site and find the answers to the following questions.

- What are three animals you might see while visiting the park?
- What are the hours the Visitor Center is open?
- What is the top layer of the Grand Canyon called?
- What river runs through the Grand Canyon?

f. Find out what the current weather conditions are at the Grand Canyon through the University of Michigan weather center. Print this frame.

g. Return to your startup home page.

h. Exit Netscape Communicator.

On Your Own

6. Another popular WWW site is TVNet. It is home to information about networks and stations, and displays listings of programs on TV that night and pointers to TV information across the Internet. TVNet's Ultimate TV List is an organized list of Internet resources on TV shows. It can guide you to information, discussions, and so on about shows. See what you can find when you use the address: http://www.tvnet.com/TVnet.html. Go to the Ultimate TV Show list page and enter the name of your favorite TV show in the text box. Go to the official home page for that show. Find out information about the show's lead actor and print the page.

7. Finding out the current news is another very popular service available on the Web. Sources include newspapers, wire services, and radio and television news programs. Use the following URLs to catch up on current news stories. Save two pages from different sources as plain text files. Open the text files using any word processor, add your name and the current date to the documents, and print them.

URL/Newspaper or Magazine

http://www.nytimes.com
  New York Times

http://www1.trib.com/NEWS/newslist.html
  List of links to U.S. and international newspapers and newswires on the Internet

http://www.sjmercury.com
  San Jose Mercury News (California)

http://www.telegraph.co.uk.
  The London Telegraph's Electronic Telegraph (United Kingdom)

http://w3.one.net/~rhill/magss.html
  Time, People, Sports Illustrated, PC Magazine, PC World

http://www.usatoday.com
  USA Today

8. Another way to use a bookmark file you have saved is to open the bookmark file in Word 97 or another word processor that accepts hypertext links. Then you can edit it to include only links you want. If you use Word 97 you can click a link in this file to start Netscape Communicator and open the page. Open the bookmark file you saved in the lab. Edit the file to include only the bookmarks of interest to you. Add the URLs of several additional sites to the bookmark file and then click a link to view the page. Save and print the bookmark file.

9. Everywhere you look you see references to WWW pages. Write down several URLs from articles in your local newspaper or that you see on TV. Start Netscape Communicator, enter the URLs to these sites and explore the sites. Save a page of interest to your data disk in plain text format. Open the text file using any word processor and add your name and the current date to the top of the page. Print the text file.

10. Select several sites described on the next page and use the URLs provided to explore the sites. Print the home page of two of the sites.

Topic	Address	Description
Boston	http://www.bostonusa.com/index.shtml	Over 1000 points of interest, event listings and descriptions, and information on Boston.
California	http://gocalif.ca.gov	California's official source of travel and tourism information.
China	http://www.ihep.ac.cn/tour/bj.html	Tour of Beijing China.
Computer games	http://www.gamesdomain.com	The Games Domain is the place to go for information on dozens of computer games. Resources include hints for specific games and an online game magazine.
Congress	http://www.lcv.org	See how your local congressperson is ranked by the League of Conservation Voters.
Congressional bills	http://thomas.loc.gov	The Library of Congress's Thomas (as in Thomas Jefferson) service lets you look up pending bills by keyword and read the *Congressional Record* (back to 1993).
Dinosaurs	http://pubs.usgs.gov/gip/dinosaurs	The Dinosaur fact and fiction site provides answers to some of your dinosaur questions.
Disney	http://www.disney.com	This is the official site for Disney.
Brewpubs of the World	http://pekkel.uthscsa.edu/Beer/Brewpub/Elsewhere/states.html	Brewpubs, microbreweries, and fine bars of the world.
Government	http://www.fedworld.gov	FedWorld is a gateway to dozens of federal information services in the U.S., some free, some requiring a fee to use.
Golf	http://www.golfdirect.com	A guide to golf real estate communities, golf resorts, golf courses, and golf schools of North America.
Legal information	http://www.law.cornell.edu/lii.table.html	Cornell University's Legal Information Institute provides a variety of law-related documents, including information on specific legal issues and copies of U.S. Supreme Court decisions.
Movies	http://sharon.kirchgruppe.de/Kirch/Text/WhatsNew/Filmo.htm	You can search for filmographies of actors and directors.
Music	http://www.music.indiana.edu/music_resources	This resource at Indiana University will help you find Web sites devoted to virtually every type of music and band.
White House	http://www.whitehouse.gov	Tours and more of the White House.
Wine	http://www.ohwy.com/wa/h/hedgecel.htm	Provides information on wineries in Washington state.

Concept Summary

████ ████ ████ ████ ████ ████ ████ ▒▒▒▒ ░░░░

Navigating the Web

1

Uniform Resource Locator

A Uniform Resource Locator (URL) provides location information that is used to navigate through the Internet to access a page.

Web Page

A Web page is a text file that has been created using a special programming language, called HyperText Markup Language, and that contains links to other Web pages and graphics.

Hypertext Link

A hypertext link, also called a hyperlink or simply a link, is a connection to another Web page or to another location on the current page.

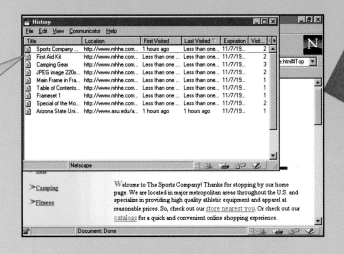

Cache

A cache is a location in your computer system that stores the page information when it is downloaded from the network.

HyperText Markup Language

All Web pages are written using a programming language called HyperText Markup Language (HTML).

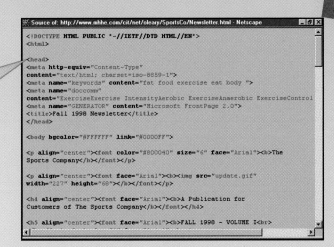

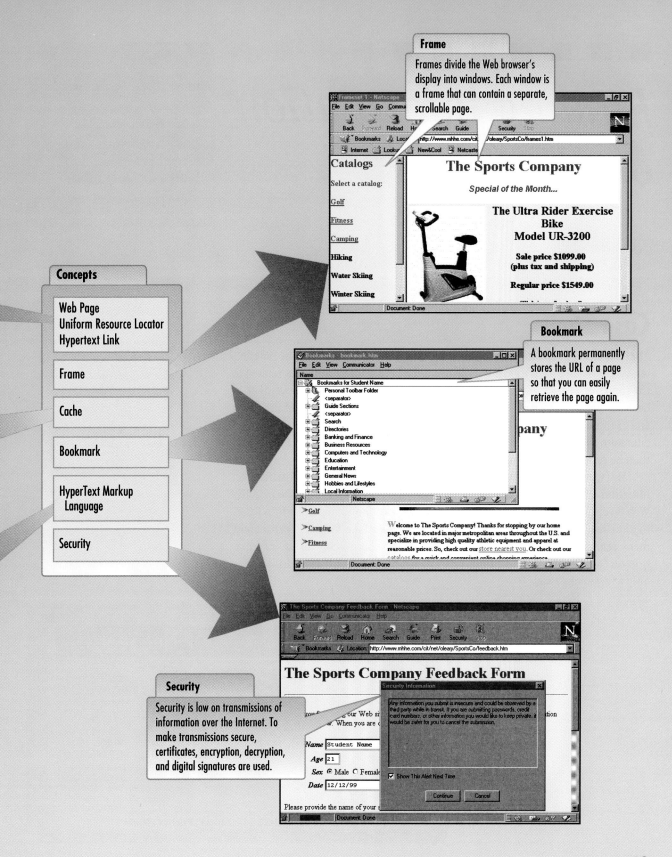

Frame

Frames divide the Web browser's display into windows. Each window is a frame that can contain a separate, scrollable page.

Concepts

Web Page
Uniform Resource Locator
Hypertext Link

Frame

Cache

Bookmark

HyperText Markup Language

Security

Bookmark

A bookmark permanently stores the URL of a page so that you can easily retrieve the page again.

Security

Security is low on transmissions of information over the Internet. To make transmissions secure, certificates, encryption, decryption, and digital signatures are used.

Finding Information on the Web

2

Case Study

After exploring The Sports Company's new Web site and looking at the newsletter, you feel that an additional Web page, containing links to Web sites related to the topics discussed in the newsletter, would be a worthwhile improvement to the site. The current newsletter consists of two general articles about nutrition and exercise. The plan for future newsletters is to include topics with more specific information about these two general areas. The page of related links could then be expanded and categorized as each newsletter is published.

You want to find articles on the Web that support the two general articles on nutrition and health. To locate this information, you could simply browse the Web by clicking on links from one location to another and hopefully find information related to these topics. However, this could take forever. Fortunately, many search services have been developed to help you quickly locate information on the Web. Using these tools you will see that finding this information is only a few clicks away.

Concept Overview

The following concepts will be introduced in this lab:

1. Search Services	Search services are huge databases of Web pages and Internet resources that are used to locate information.
2. Basic Search Methods	The two basic means of searching are by navigating through topic lists or by entering a keyword or phrase into a search text box.
3. Advanced Search Methods	To further refine your keyword searches, you can use Boolean operators, special words that indicate a relationship among keywords in a search.
4. Metasearch Engine	A metasearch engine is a search utility that submits your query to several search engines simultaneously.

Finding Search Services

- Start Netscape Communicator.

- To allow more information to appear in the content area, hide the Personal toolbar.

To find information on the WWW, you could select hypertext links that lead you from one related topic and location to another. After many selections and possible diversions, you may finally reach your destination. If you have plenty of time and are just exploring, this is fine. But what if you want to quickly locate information about a specific topic? As the Web has grown, many Web indexing services have developed that provide search services to help you find information.

Concept 1: Search Services

Search services are huge databases of Web pages and Internet resources that are used to locate information. A search is conducted by entering keywords or by browsing topic lists. The search service generates a listing of documents containing the keywords or that are related to the topic you have selected. In addition, some search services use concept search technology that looks for the ideas most closely linked to the words describing what you are looking for. This increases your chances of finding what you want on the first try.

Search services can be categorized into two types: Web directories and search engines. **Web directories**, also referred to as Web Guides, are databases that organize the sites by topics or subjects. Some directories offer reviews and ratings of the sites. Most directories are also searchable, meaning you can enter a query, or a written search request, to find sites that contain the keyword you specify. Editorial staff continually add sites to the database and gladly accept suggestions from users.

Search engines also maintain databases of Web sites but typically offer no editorial content or categories. They use a "spider" (also called a Web crawler, robot, bot, harvester, or worm) to check out Web sites, reading and storing keywords and links and adding new sites to their existing database. The spider periodically connects to servers to update its database. Different search engines use spiders that may search for different keywords in the pages. Therefore, if you conducted the same search using different search engines, the results would probably be different. Search engines typically are faster and provide a more comprehensive list of results than directories because no human intervention is needed and spiders cover much more of the Web. On the downside, the list is not typically categorized or reviewed.

Because no one search service has all the Web pages on the Web in its index, and because the search services use different techniques and search different types of Web resources, it is advisable to use more than one engine when conducting a search. It is also helpful to know which tools may be best suited to find the type of information you need. The following table provides a brief description of many of the most popular search services. All URLs begin with http://www.

Web Directory	URL	Description
Yahoo	yahoo.com	Large index of hand-selected pages grouped by categories.
NetGuide	netguide.com	Over 50,000 reviewed and categorized sites.
Lycos PointCom	point.com	Contains an index of the top 5% of pretested and quality-checked sites in the Lycos database.
Lycos A2Z	a2z.lycos.com	Categorized directory of the most popular Internet resources in the Lycos database.
LookSmart	looksmart.com	New search directory backed by the *Reader's Digest* includes more than 250,000 reviewed sites that are organized into 12,500 categories.
Magellan	mckinley.com	Reviewed and rated sites. Good family site.

Search Engine	URL	Description
Excite	excite.com	Searches over 50 million indexed Web pages, or 65,000 reviewed sites. Fast, big search engine with site reviews and travel guides. Uses concept search technology and relevancy ranking.
Infoseek	infoseek.com	Fast, easy-to-use search engine and directory with site reviews. Over 50 million pages on Web. The recommended Infoseek Select Sites are designated with a checkmark.
Lycos	lycos.com	A large database that includes site's URL, title, and first 20 lines from which it automatically generates an abstract.
Alta Vista	altavista.digital.com	One of the largest and fastest search engines. No selection or ranking process. Generates list of pages, not sites. Best place if trying to find obscure piece of information.
AOL NetFind	aol.com/netfind	Uses concept search technology.
WebCrawler	webcrawler.com	America Online's resident WWW site catalog. Small but easy to use. Includes reviewed sites.
HotBot	hotbot.com	Fast, though small, search engine.

When looking for information on a general topic, use a directory such as Yahoo to start your search. If you are looking for a specific concept or phrase, or something that is not easily categorized, use a search engine such as Alta Vista, Lycos, or Infoseek to get comprehensive listings.

There are many different means to access the different search services. The most direct method is to type in the URL or to select the bookmark for the search service you want to use. However, until you are familiar with the different search services and find those that you like using best, you will probably access a Web page that provides links to the search services.

Commonly, many startup home pages include a link to a page that provides a list of links to many search services. Another way is to go to a Web site that offers listings of search service resources. One resource is C/Net's SEARCH.COM site (http://www.search.com). This site is a compilation of just about all the search services on the Web. It provides a one-stop resource to search services and even includes a description of each tool. Another is the All-in-One Search Page (http://www.albany.net/allinone), which contains a huge collection of search and reference tools. In addition, Netscape provides its own page of search services and a button to quickly access it. To use this page,

■   Click   [Search]

Your screen should be similar to Figure 2-1.

> C/Net is the computer network that integrates television programming with a network of WWW sites.

> The menu equivalent is **E**dit/Search **I**nternet.

FIGURE 2-1

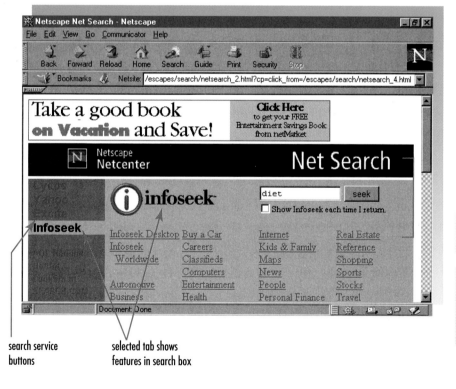

search service buttons

selected tab shows features in search box

> Your NetSearch page may have a different selected search service.

> Because Web sites are always adding features and redesigning their pages, the screens in this lab may not exactly match what you see.

At the top of the page are nine buttons that display the names of different search services. The highlighted tab button shows the selected tool whose features are displayed in the Search box below.

Below the Search box is a list of additional search services categorized by capability.

The Customize link is used to select one of the five services to add to the tabs.

■   Scroll the page to see the list of other search services below the Search box.

Your screen should be similar to Figure 2-2.

FIGURE 2-2

additional search
services categorized
by type

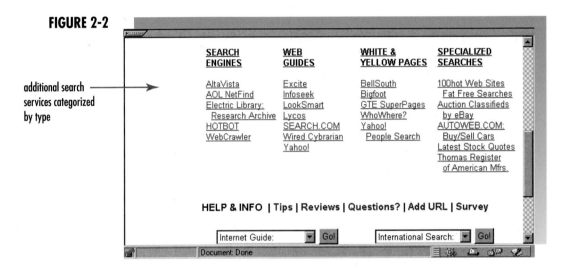

You will use Yahoo, one of the original search services developed, to help you locate information.

■   Scroll back to the top of the page.

■   If necessary, click **Yahoo** .

Your screen should be similar to Figure 2-3.

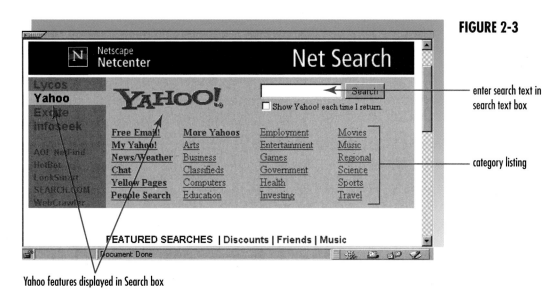

FIGURE 2-3

enter search text in
search text box

category listing

Yahoo features displayed in Search box

The Search box now reflects Yahoo's features. It includes a search text box and
Yahoo's top-level category listing.

Searching by Topic

Depending upon the type of search service you are using, there are two basic
ways to find information: searching by topic or by keyword.

Concept 2: Basic Search Methods

The two basic means of searching are by navigating through topic lists or by entering a keyword or phrase into a search text box. Some search services offer both methods, others only one.

Use the **topic search** when you are looking for general information. Using this method you navigate through a hierarchy of topic listings that group the items in the database into subject categories, such as art, business, and sports. The main subject groupings are further categorized into subtopics; for example the sports group may have subdivisions of cycling, baseball, and soccer. As you continue to make selections from the topic groups, you narrow the number of listings that will be available to those that more precisely match the information you are seeking.

If you are looking for a specific concept or a phrase, use the **keyword search** method. The search program compares this text with some part of the text it has stored in its database—title, URL, text, a description, abstract, or review—then displays a list of all pages in its database that contain the text you specified.

Some simple tips for finding what you want using keywords:

1. Be specific. Use more descriptive, specific words as opposed to general ones. The more descriptive the keyword you enter, the better your results.

2. Use multiple words. You may want to use synonyms to help narrow the field of your search.

3. Leave out nonessential words like prepositions and articles; most search programs ignore them anyway.

If the search yields too few results or "hits," your keyword may be too specific or may include incorrect terms. Try again using different or less specific words. Conversely, if you get too many hits, you may want to narrow the field by using more specific words.

Since the articles in the newsletter provide general information about nutrition and fitness, you want to begin by finding several sites that provide general advice on these topics, rather than information about a specific topic. To do this, you will perform a topic search.

■   Click Health.

Your screen should be similar to Figure 2-4.

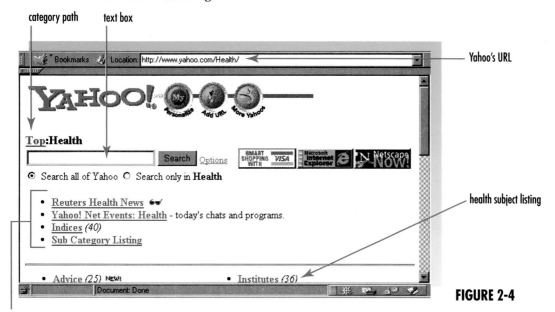

FIGURE 2-4

After a few moments, a new page containing links to health topics is loaded. Notice from the URL that you are no longer at Netscape's Net Search page, but are at Yahoo's Web site.

Note: If you receive a message indicating you cannot connect to a site, it may be that the maximum number of users is accessing the location. Resubmit your request several times and you will probably get on. If not, skip to the next section, "Searching by Keyword," on page 55 and return to this section later.

Above the text box is the path of category selections you have made. In this case, you started at the home page (Top) and selected the Health category, the currently displayed page. Clicking on the Top link will return you directly to the first page.

Below the text box are several links to suggested health-related services offered by Yahoo. Below this is another subject list.

■ Scroll the page to see the subject list.

Your screen should be similar to Figure 2-5.

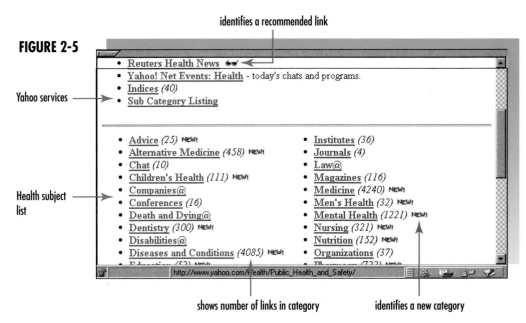

FIGURE 2-5

This subject listing contains only health-related topics. Yahoo categorizes links to Web pages starting with general categories, with each subcategory increasingly more specific. The parentheses next to each subject listing indicate the number of links included in that category. An @ symbol means the link goes to a different Yahoo category. New categories are also identified with the **NEW!** symbol. Links with 👓 mean these links are recommended.

Since the newsletter articles briefly discuss activities to improve fitness, you want to refer readers to Web sites on this topic. This category contains approximately 100 links (at the time of this writing) to Web pages related to Fitness.

■ Scroll the subject list and click <u>Fitness</u>.

This page includes another listing of fitness subcategories as well as a listing of links to Web resources related to health and fitness. The path of selections you have made is extended to include your most recent selection (<u>Top</u>:<u>Health</u>:<u>Fitness</u>). The previously selected category is now a link back to that page.

■ Scroll the page to see the subject listing of fitness topics, followed by a listing of links to Web pages on fitness.

Your screen should be similar to Figure 2-6.

listing of fitness categories   description of Web site

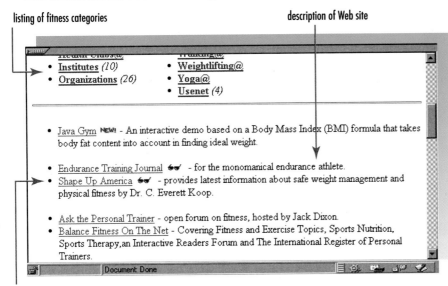

Web resource links

FIGURE 2-6

Your screen may display different sites as new ones are added and old ones removed.

Each item in the list consists of the page title as a hypertext link to the site and a brief description of the site. In addition, if the Yahoo staff has reviewed a site, clicking the ▸REVIEW◂ icon will display the review.

The description of the Shape Up America site appears to cover content similar to the articles in this month's newsletter. To check out this site,

■   Click <u>Shape Up America</u>.

Your screen should be similar to Figure 2-7.

FIGURE 2-7

The Shape Up America home page is downloaded. To further check out the contents of this site,

■   Scroll the page and click <u>Health & Fitness</u>.

This page looks interesting. It provides a link to an assessment of your fitness level as well as links to basic information about fitness and different types of physical activity.

■ Click <u>Assess Your Fitness Level</u>.

You think this looks like a good site for inclusion in the newsletter-related links page and decide to create a bookmark to the site's home page.

■ Return to the site's home page (use the <u>Shape Up America!</u> link at the bottom of the page).

■ Create a bookmark to the page.

■ Use the Go menu to return to the Yahoo Health:Fitness page of topics.

As you continue your search for sites related to the newsletter articles, you want to create a list of the sites to give your supervisor. To do this, you can copy the site description to a word processor document.

> To highlight the description, drag when the mouse pointer is an I-beam.

> Use Start/**P**rograms/Accessories to load WordPad.

> You could use any word processor program on your system.

■ Select the Shape Up America link and site description.

■ Copy the selection to the Clipboard (**E**dit/**C**opy or Ctrl + C).

■ Open WordPad and click 🔲 to paste the selection into a new document window.

Your screen should be similar to Figure 2-8.

pastes Clipboard contents

FIGURE 2-8

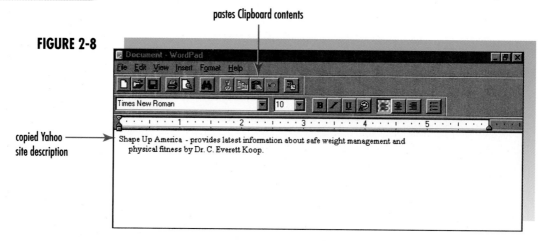

copied Yahoo site description

In addition, you want to copy the site's URL to the WordPad document.

> Use the taskbar button to switch applications.

■ Switch to Netscape and click Forward to display the Shape Up America! home page again.

■ Click in the Location text box and copy the selection to the WordPad document following the description.

■ Switch back to Netscape and go to several other sites from the Yahoo! Health:Fitness page list. When you have found another good site, bookmark it and copy the description and URL to the WordPad document.

■ Switch back to Netscape.

Searching by Keyword

Next you will conduct a search by entering keywords in a search text box. The first article in the newsletter discusses the basics of eating a healthy diet. You will use the Infoseek search service to locate information on this topic.

- Use the Go menu to return to the Netscape Net Search page.

- Click **Infoseek**.

- Click in the search text box and type **diet**.

- Click **seek**.

search text box

Your screen should be similar to Figure 2-9.

number of Web pages in index text that contain keyword

FIGURE 2-9

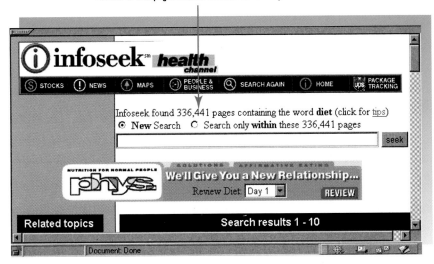

After a few moments, Infoseek shows how many pages it located that contain the keyword "diet" and displays the first page of search results.

- Scroll the page to see the first few pages in the results list.

Your search will most likely display a different number of pages.

Your screen should be similar to Figure 2-10.

first page of Infoseek search
results of using keyword: diet

content summary

FIGURE 2-10

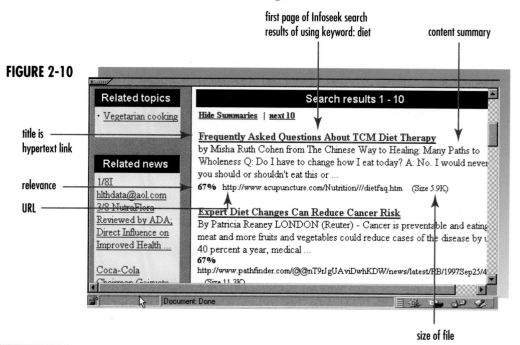

title is
hypertext link

relevance

URL

size of file

Your list of search results will be
different from Figure 2-10.

Infoseek displays 10 search results at a time. Each result includes a title that is a hypertext link to the page containing the keywords, a content summary commonly consisting of the first few lines of text on the page, the URL of the Web page, and the size of the file. In addition, Infoseek displays a percent value that indicates how relevant the site is to your keyword search. A site gets a higher percentage rating if the keyword is found in the title or near the start of the document, if the number of times the keyword is found in the document is more than others, and if the document contains a keyword that is relatively uncommon in the database. The highest rated sites are listed first.

■ Scroll the page and read several of the search results.

■ Click the <u>Next 10</u> link at the top or bottom of the search result list to see the next full page of search results.

■ Scroll the list of results and click <u>Prev 10</u> to return to the previous page.

After quickly checking out the first two pages of search results, you see that the sites mostly link to pages about weight loss and diet products rather than to information about nutrition. You decide to change the search keyword to locate information on nutrition. Notice that Infoseek has a Search text box at the top and bottom of each page in which you can specify a new search (the default) or you can refine your current search by restricting the new search to the located documents.

■ Move to the Search box at the top of the page.

■ Type **nutrition information** in the text box.

■ Click seek .

■ Scroll the page to see the beginning of the search results list.

Your screen should be similar to Figure 2-11.

FIGURE 2-11

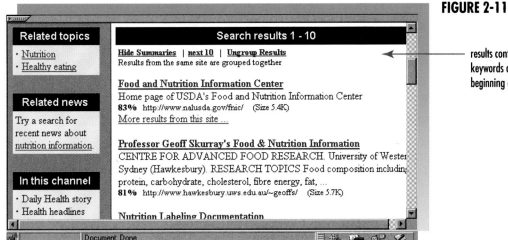

results containing both keywords appear at the beginning of the results list

When you enter multiple words, Infoseek displays Web pages containing all the words in your query at the top of the results list. This feature broadens your search, much as if you had navigated through the topic list, but a lot faster. Generally, the longer the keyword query, the better the results. If you know the specific type of information you are looking for, it is more efficient to use a keyword search rather than a topic search.

These search results appear to provide information more related to the topics discussed in the newsletter.

■ Click the link to the USDA's <u>Food and Nutrition Information Center</u> and explore the site.

Again, this site appears to have good basic information on this topic.

■ Bookmark the Food and Nutrition Information Center home page.

■ Copy the Infoseek site description and URL to the WordPad document.

■ Switch back to Netscape and go to several other sites from the Infoseek search results list. When you have found another good site, bookmark it and copy the description to the WordPad document.

If the Food and Nutrition Information Center site is not listed, select another site of your choice.

Advanced Searches

As you can see, when conducting a keyword search, you can get search results that more closely match your needs by entering a more specific keyword or by using several related keywords. In addition, you can use the advanced search features.

Concept 3: Advanced Search Methods

To further refine your keyword searches, you can use **Boolean operators**—or find modifiers like AND, OR, and NOT and parentheses. These operators must appear in ALL CAPS and with a space on each side in order to work. They allow you to combine keywords to include the information you want and to eliminate other information. The Boolean operators as well as several other commonly used advanced search features and their effects are described in the table below.

Operator	Effect
AND (or &)	Documents found must contain all words joined by the word AND. The AND operator is assumed by many search services.
	Example: *rock AND roll AND music* finds articles on rock and roll music.
+ (plus sign)	Specifies that each word preceded with a + must appear on each page in the result list. Put the plus sign directly in front of the word you want included, with no spaces.
	Example: *+rock +roll +music* finds articles with all three words, whereas *rock +roll +music* will include roll and music, but not necessarily rock.
OR (or |)	Documents must contain at least one of the words connected by OR.
- (minus sign)	Specifies that words preceded with a - cannot appear in the search results. Put the minus sign directly in front of the word you want left out, with no spaces.
	Example: *+billiards -equipment -supplies* finds articles with the word billiards but not equipment or supplies.
NOT (or !)	Excludes words—similar to the minus sign effect—but must be used with the operators AND or OR as in AND NOT or OR NOT.
	Example: To find articles about pets, excluding cats, enter *pets AND NOT cats*, or *pets !cats*.
NEAR (or ~)	Specifies two words that must appear close together in the same page.
	Example: To find articles on wolves that have been domesticated, enter *wolves~domesticated*.
" (quotation marks)	Finds only exact multiple word phrases, whereas not using quotes finds documents containing any of those words, anywhere on the document, in any order.
	Example: *Air Force 1* finds only documents with this exact phrase.
( )	Used to group portions of Boolean queries together for more complicated searches.
	Example: *pets AND (cats OR birds)* finds pages with the word pets and either the word cats or birds.
* (wildcard)	Indicates any amount of letters or symbols.
	Example: Entering *air** would find pages that contain words like airmail, airplane, airport, and airspeed.

Some other ways to make your searches more accurate are:

- Limit the scope of the search by specifying an area of the database to search, such as a topic category, newsgroups, e-mail, or mailing lists.
- Use a search feature that looks for whole words only or pieces of the words.
- Use a search feature to find all keywords with or without regard to case.
- Some search services include a "more like this" link next to the result article link. Clicking this link instructs the search engine to use that document as an example of what else to look for, to find more sites similar to the one you liked.
- Another search service feature you may see allows you to enter a revised keyword query that will expand or narrow your search results. Look for a Refine Your Find or Search These Results link.

Because the advanced search features vary with the search service you are using, it is a good idea to check out each search service's page of information on conducting advanced searches and tips that explain its particular features and give you more control over how the search is conducted.

Next you want to find information specifically about the food guide pyramid that is discussed in the newsletter article. We will use the Excite search service to locate this information using some advanced search features.

- Use the Go menu to return to the Netscape Net Search page.
- Click **Excite** .
- Click in the Search text box and type **pyramid**
- Click **Search** .
- Scroll the page to see the first few search results.

Your screen should be similar to Figure 2-12.

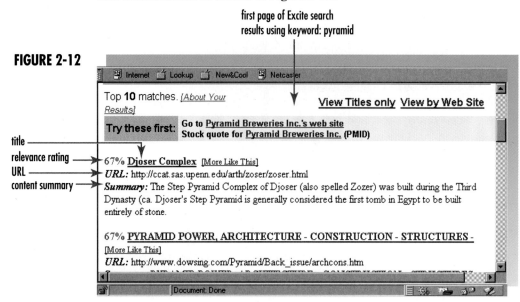

FIGURE 2-12

Excite also lists 10 search results at a time on a page. Each result includes a relevance rating (%), the title and URL, and a brief summary of the content. The most relevant documents are listed first.

■ Scroll the list and notice the variety of topics included in the search results.

Notice that many of the results do not have anything to do with food or nutrition guidelines. This is because all sites that contain the word "pyramid" are listed. This includes sites that sell pyramid-shaped pet houses, Egyptian pyramids, and so on. To make the search more accurate, you will modify the search query to include the word "food" and exclude the word "Egypt."

■ Display the Search text box at the bottom of the page.

In addition to a Search box at the top and bottom of each page, Excite also includes a list of related words. You can click on a word to add it to your search query to help you identify exactly what it is about the particular topic that you are interested in locating. In this case however, none of the words are appropriate. To refine your search,

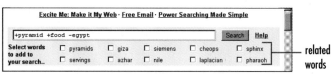

Many search services include a feature that allows you to select advanced search options from list boxes rather than to have to type the sequence in the correct format in the Search text box. Excite's is accessed using the Power Search link.

■ Edit the keyword search to **+pyramid +food -egypt**.

■ Click Search .

■ Scroll the page to see the search results.

Your screen should be similar to Figure 2-13.

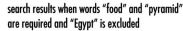

search results when words "food" and "pyramid"
are required and "Egypt" is excluded

FIGURE 2-13

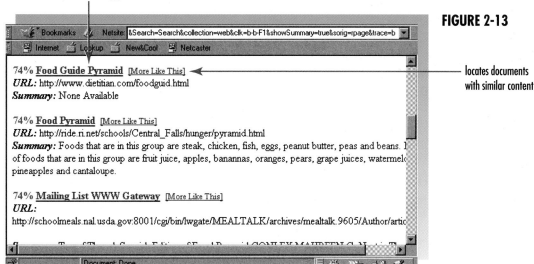

locates documents
with similar content

Now only sites that include the word "pyramid" or "food" but not "Egypt" are included in the search results. Also, notice that Excite includes a More Like This link with each result. This feature instructs the search engine to use the content of that document as an example in a new search to find more sites similar to the one you liked.

■ Click the <u>More Like This</u> link of any search result that refers to the Food Guide Pyramid.

■ Scroll the list of related sites.

The results much more closely match the type of information you need. Perhaps the most effective search would have been to enter the phrase "food guide pyramid" in quotes as the search query. To see what the results would be using this phrase,

■ Enter **"food guide pyramid"** in the search text box.

■ Click Search .

■ Scroll the page to see the first few listed results.

Your screen should be similar to Figure 2-14.

FIGURE 2-14

results contain exact
phrase specified in
search query

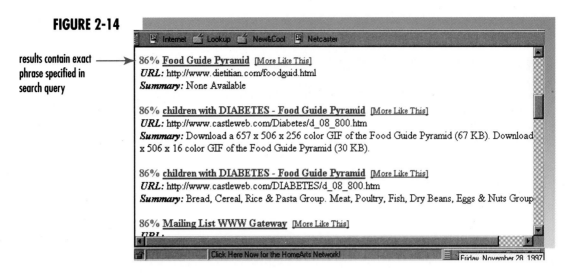

All the sites included in the results contain the exact phrase you specified, making the search results right on the mark.

■ Explore several of the sites from the Excite search results list. When you have found another good site, bookmark it and copy the description to the WordPad document.

■ Switch back to Netscape.

As you can see, using the advanced search features greatly helps to refine your search to locate documents that are as close as possible to the content you are seeking. Even the order you enter the words in the query has an effect on the results. If you were to perform the same search using different search services, you would see many of the same search results. But each search service will include sites that were not included by the others. For this reason, even if you find you have a favorite search service, it is advisable to check several to do a more thorough search.

Using a Metasearch Engine

As you can imagine, searching using several search engines in sequence is tedious and produces many duplicate hits. This problem has been largely overcome by the development of search utilities called metasearch engines.

Concept 4: Metasearch Engine

A **metasearch engine** is a search utility that submits your query to several search engines simultaneously. Like a standard search engine, you enter keywords. The list of results is usually ordered by relevance with all the duplicates removed. It then lets you repeat the search by selecting other search engines or by modifying your keyword query. The major benefit to users of metasearch engines is the increased speed of conducting and modifying searches and of scanning the search results.

Many of these search utilities are available online for free. Others are utility programs that you can purchase that will conduct the same type of search as the online metasearch engines with fewer restrictions. Several of the online metasearch engines and the utility programs you can purchase are listed in the tables below.

Online Engine	URL
SavvySearch	guaraldi.cs.colostate.edu:2000/form
SavvySearch Version 2	SavvySearch version 2 is currently under development and offers many enhancements over the original version. guaraldi.cs.colostate.edu:2000/form?beta
MetaCrawler	metacrawler.com
FerretSoft's WebFerret	ferretsoft.com

Utility Program	URL
BitSafe Computer Services Arf	dwave.net./~bitsafe/arf/index.html
ForeFront Group's WebSeeker	ffg.com
Symantec's Internet FastFind	symantec.com
Quarterdeck's WebCompass	quarterdeck.com

Other terms for this type of search utility include search consolidators, simultaneous search engines, multiple search devices, multi-threader search tools, parallel search engines, and multi-threaded engines.

Netscape's Net Search page as of this writing does not include any of the metasearch engines.

- Use one of the search services to locate the SavvySearch metasearch engine, or enter the URL **http://guaraldi.cs.colostate.edu:2000/form** to go directly to the site.

- If necessary, display SavvySearch's Search Form.

Your screen should be similar to Figure 2-15.

FIGURE 2-15

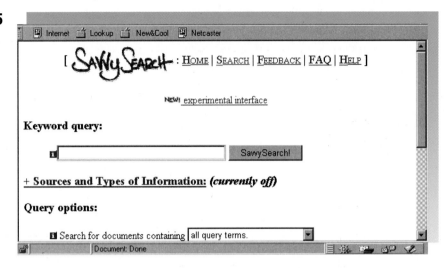

The SavvySearch site is often busy, indicating that there are insufficient computing resources for the service's query load—a common problem with newly popular resources on the Internet.

You will use SavvySearch to search for information on the benefits of exercise as discussed in the second newsletter article. Below the text box are the search option settings.

- If necessary, click <u>Sources and Types of Information</u> to display the list of options.

- In the Search text box type **exercise "weight loss"**

- Scroll the page to see the list of sources and options.

Your screen should be similar to Figure 2-16.

FIGURE 2-16

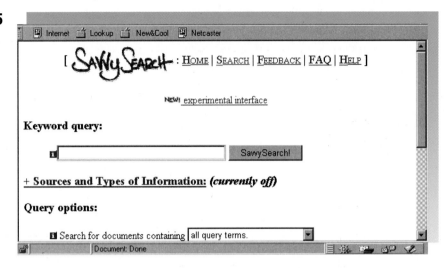

The Sources and Types of Information link opens a list of categories you can select to limit your search to specific areas of the Internet. The WWW Resources option is selected by default. The query options can be used to refine the search. By default they are set to require that all search terms are included in the search result documents, to display 10 hits from each search engine, and to display a normal amount of description.

If you are using the SavvySearch Version 2, the listing of Sources and Types of Information appears immediately below the Search text box rather than as a link.

- To start the search using the default search settings, click SavvySearch! .

- Scroll the results list to the bottom of the page.

Your screen should be similar to Figure 2-17.

FIGURE 2-17

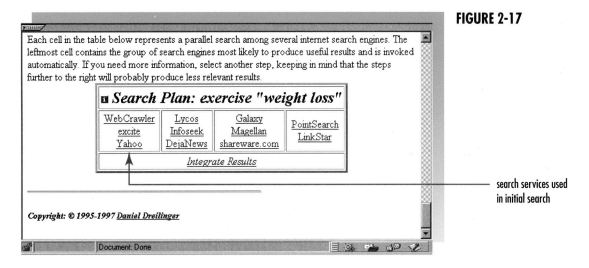

search services used
in initial search

The search results from three search services are listed. The search services are selected based on an analysis of such factors as the content of the submitted query and the current response times of the search services. At the bottom of the page is a table that displays the services in groups of three. The first group contains the three services that SavvySearch felt were most likely to produce the results you wanted and were used to conduct the initial search. You can select a different group of search services on which you can run your search by clicking the appropriate cell of the table.

- Select links to several of the search results listed.

- Bookmark two sites and copy the description and if necessary the URL of these sites to the WordPad document.

- Enter your name and the current date at the top of the WordPad document. Save the WordPad document to your data disk as Newsletter Links. Print the document. Close the file and exit WordPad.

- Save your bookmark list to your data disk and remove the bookmarks you added in Navigator.

Finding People and Businesses

Another source of information are databases, commonly called the **white** and **yellow pages**, that are used to search for people or businesses. It used to be that the only way to locate people and businesses was through the traditional printed white and yellow pages and through telephone directory assistance. Now, these same services and more are offered by online search services. Many of these services also provide phone and mail address information, in addition to e-mail addresses.

> You will learn about e-mail addresses in Lab 3.

Although the best way is still to ask the computer user directly, by telephone or through mutual friends, there are times when this is not possible. To help locate people and businesses, you can also use one of the following utility programs.

> The URL begins with http://www unless otherwise noted.

White Pages	URL
LookUp USAPeople Directory	lookupusa.com/lookupusa/adp/ peopsrch.html
Switchboard	switchboard.com
BigFoot	bigfoot.com
Four11	four11.com
WhoWhere	whowhere.com
Populus	populus.net

Yellow Pages	URL
Big Book	bigbook.com
US West Dex	yp.uswest.com
GTE SuperPages®	superpages.com
Switchboard	switchboard.com

To quickly locate many of these sites, you can use the Netscape button.

■   Click .

The Guide menu contains five options that access Netscape's pages containing links to Internet information. The People option contains links to white pages indexes.

■   Click People.

Your screen should be similar to Figure 2-18.

FIGURE 2-18

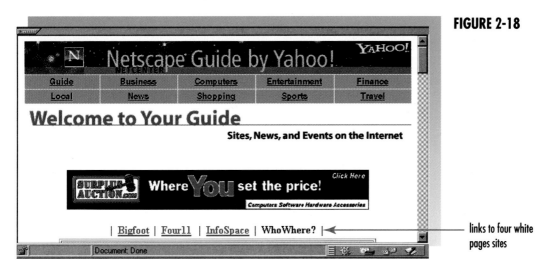

links to four white pages sites

Much like the Net Search page, the People Guide page contains links to four white pages sites and a Search box. The selected white pages link appears in black text, and the Search box displays the features needed to conduct a search using that site. You will use the InfoSpace white pages site to search for a person's e-mail address by entering the requested information in the search text boxes.

- If necessary, click InfoSpace.

- Enter the following information in the appropriate text boxes of the Find E-mail Addresses section of the form:

  First name: leave blank

  Last name: **Brown**

  Enter your city and state in the appropriate boxes.

- Click Find It.

- Scroll the page to view the first few results.

> Use Edit/Search Directory to open the Search dialog box to perform a white pages search.

> You can also use InfoSpace to find phone numbers.

Your screen should be similar to Figure 2-19.

FIGURE 2-19

located people

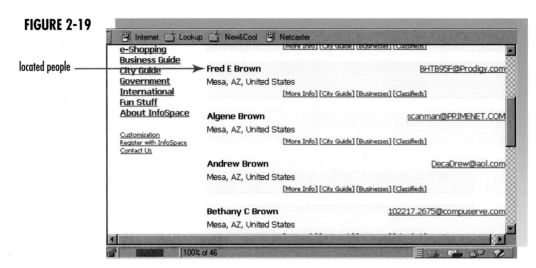

A list of those people with last names of Brown in your city and state is displayed. Of course, the more specific you can make your search request, the fewer matches will be located.

The procedure to search using the yellow pages is much the same except that only business sites are included in the site's database.

■ Continue to search for other people or businesses of your choice.

■ When you are done, exit Netscape Communicator.

LAB REVIEW

■ ■ ■ ■ ■ ■ ■ ■ ■ ■ ■ ■

Key Terms

Boolean operator   (NET58)   topic search   (NET50)
keyword search   (NET50)   Web directory   (NET45)
metasearch engine   (NET63)   white pages   (NET66)
search engine   (NET45)   yellow pages   (NET66)
search service   (NET45)

Command Summary

Command	Button	Action
Edit/Search **I**nternet		Displays Netscape Net Search page
Edit/Search Director**y**		Opens Search dialog box

Matching

1. keyword   _____   **a.** Boolean operator to find all words joined by the operator

2. Yahoo   _____   **b.** word used to locate pages that contain specific information

3. Web directory   _____   **c.** search engine that displays pages, not sites

4. AND   _____   **d.** search utility that submits query to several search engines

5. search engine   _____   **e.** databases of categorized sites that are compiled by people

6. Alta Vista   _____   **f.** Boolean operator to find one of the words joined by the operator

7. yellow pages   _____   **g.** uses a spider to locate Web sites

8. OR   _____   **h.** database that contains people's phone numbers and e-mail addresses

9. metasearch   _____   **i.** Web directory

10. white pages   _____   **j.** database that contains business phone numbers and e-mail addresses

Discussion Questions

1. Describe the two types of search services. Explain why you would want to use more than one search service to locate information.

2. Discuss three basic procedures you can use to make your keyword searches more effective.

3. Discuss five advanced search procedures.

4. How can you find someone's e-mail address?

Hands-On Practice Exercises

Step by Step

Rating System		
	☆	Easy
	☆☆	Moderate
	☆☆☆	Difficult

1. In this problem, you will learn more about how to conduct searches using different search services.

   a. Open the Netscape Net Search page.

   b. Select the <u>Tips</u> link.

   c. Read the search tips associated with the selected search service.

   d. Select a different search service under <u>Tips</u> on this page to learn about the search features associated with that service.

   e. Select several other search services and read the tips.

   f. List three search tips that are commonly found in all search services. How does Excite differ from the other search services?

   g. Read and print the Dummies Daily Tip.

2. Using a search service of your choice, locate a picture of the Mona Lisa. Write down the URL for the picture location. Download the graphic file. Print the picture.

3. In this problem you will use another white pages service to find e-mail addresses.

   a. Open the Netscape People Guide search page.

   b. Using the Four11 white pages, search for your name. Did you find yourself?

   c. If you found yourself, you have registered previously for this service. If you did not find yourself, click Add Me. Follow the directions on the screen to add your name and personal information to the service. As of this writing, this is a free service that will help friends and family locate your e-mail address.

   d. Use the Four11 white pages to search for e-mail addresses for friends and family.

4. You are planning to rent a movie at the local video store and want to check out several movie reviews on the Web before you go.

   a. Using a search service of your choice, find a movie review for a recent movie on video. Print the review.

   b. Save the search service's description and the URL to a WordPad document.

   c. Use a different search service to locate a movie review for an old movie (more than 10 years old). Print the review.

   d. Save the search service's description and the URL to the WordPad document.

   e. Using Yahoo, perform a topic search to locate a Web site that reviews current movies. Print a review of a current movie.

   f. Add your name and the current date to the WordPad document. Print the document.

On your Own

5. You may need to travel at some point during your career. The Internet Travel Network lets you track fares and prices on domestic airlines. The system automatically displays the lowest available fare for an itinerary and can be used to book reservations and send tickets to the user. This is a free service but has a charge for booking tickets. Locate this service and establish an account. Check prices for a trip you would like to take. Check several airlines and find the lowest price available.

6. You are preparing a paper for a course in your field of study. Use Netscape to locate three text files that contain information on the topic of your paper. Copy and paste the page title and URLs to a word processor document. Include a brief summary of the information in the text files. Locate two pictures that may be useful in the paper. Save the pictures to your data disk. Add your name to the text document. Print the text file of descriptions and URLs along with the two pictures.

7. Using a search service of your choice, search on San Francisco or a city of your choice and locate information on hotel accommodations. Locate pages that allow you to locate hotel rooms in the city by price, location, type of hotel, and so on. Locate photographs of hotel lobbies and rooms. If possible, locate pages that allow you to check availability. After checking out three hotels, which one would you recommend staying in and why?

8. How people work has changed dramatically with the introduction of computers. As a consequence, many health-related side effects such as repetitive motion injuries commonly occur. Conduct a search for information about this topic. Write a brief paper about computer-related ergonomic problems. Include several suggestions on solutions. Using the information you found, analyze your workspace. What changes can you make to your workspace to make it ergonomically safe? Include the changes you made to your workspace in your report. Print the report.

Search Services

Search services are huge databases of Web pages and Internet resources that are used to locate information.

Metasearch Engine

A metasearch engine is a search utility that submits your query to several search engines simultaneously.

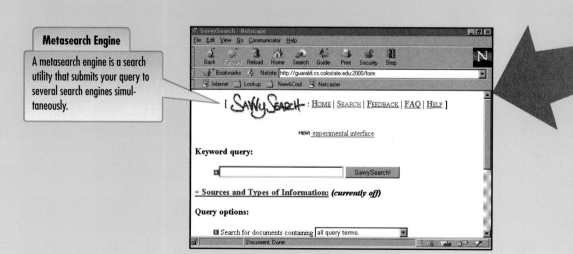

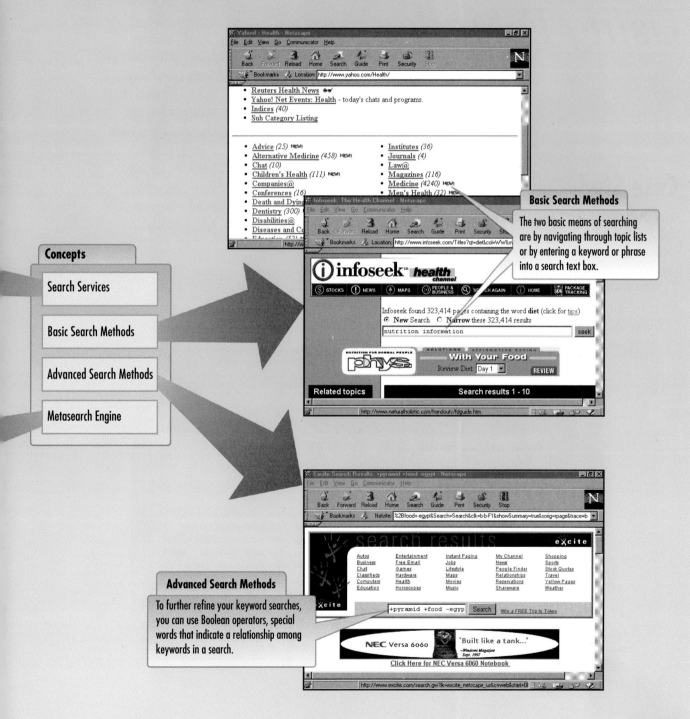

Concepts

Search Services

Basic Search Methods

Advanced Search Methods

Metasearch Engine

Basic Search Methods

The two basic means of searching are by navigating through topic lists or by entering a keyword or phrase into a search text box.

Advanced Search Methods

To further refine your keyword searches, you can use Boolean operators, special words that indicate a relationship among keywords in a search.

Corresponding Using E-Mail

Case Study

Over the past few days, you have been looking at The Sports Company Web site and considering how changes could be made to improve the newsletter. Your main suggestion is to add a page of links to fitness and nutrition topics related to the content of the articles in the newsletter.

You decide to send an e-mail message (shown below) to the regional manager explaining your suggestion, along with a copy of the Web sites you have located that would complement the current edition of the newsletter.

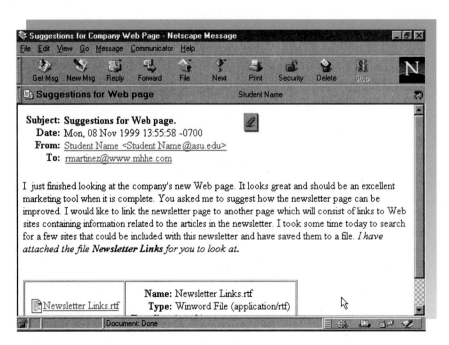

The following concepts will be introduced in this lab:

1. How E-Mail Works	E-mail requires the use of two programs: a mailer program and a delivery system.
2. E-Mail Address	On the Internet, each person has a unique e-mail address or means of identification.
3. Mail Servers	Two types of mail servers work together to handle incoming and outgoing e-mail messages.
4. Folder	A folder is an area on your disk that is used to organize and store messages.
5. Parts of an E-Mail Message	An e-mail message consists of two basic parts, the header and the body.
6. E-Mail Style and Netiquette	E-mail is a fairly new way of communicating and has developed its own style and set of rules of courteous electronic communications called Netiquette (net etiquette).
7. Address Book	Rather than trying to remember many different e-mail addresses, you can create a file of e-mail addresses called an address book.

What Is E-Mail?

The ability to communicate with others over the Internet is one of the prime reasons for its success and popularity. One of the original forms of communicating on the Internet is electronic mail or **e-mail**. E-mail allows individuals to send and receive written messages via computer.

Concept 1: How E-Mail Works

E-mail requires the use of two programs. The first is the e-mail software program, more frequently called a **mailer** or **reader program**. The mailer program provides the means of creating, sending, and reading e-mail messages. The mailer software in Netscape Communicator is called **Messenger**. There are many other e-mail programs, such as Eudora, Pegasus Mail, and Microsoft Internet Mail, that perform the same function as Messenger. A mailer program deposits the e-mail message you send in an electronic **mailbox**, which is located on a computer called a **mail server**, at your school, your work, or your Internet service provider. Each user is assigned a private mailbox when they establish an e-mail account. The mailbox is identified with the user's Internet e-mail address.

The second program is the delivery system that routes the e-mail message over the Internet to the intended recipient. As the message travels, it passes from one mail server to another until it reaches its destination, where it is placed in the recipient's mailbox.

E-mail uses **store-and-forward** technology. This means that if the recipient's computer is not available for mail delivery, the store-and-forward feature enables applications to hold messages or information for later delivery. Stored messages are then automatically forwarded when network contact is reestablished.

You will learn about e-mail addresses shortly.

INTERNET

E-mail is the main means of communication between Internet users, with more than 3 billion e-mail messages sent over the Internet each month, a six-fold increase in two years. Today, with 60 million Americans having access to e-mail, and 12.8 million U.S. households using e-mail from home, it is the most widely used application on the Internet. It is estimated that by the year 2005, more than 5 billion personal messages will be sent each day.

One reason for e-mail's growing popularity is the change in the workplace from central offices to home or on-the-road offices. E-mail provides a convenient communications pathway to co-workers and customers and allows computer users to exchange information and data files directly with one another. Another reason is that e-mail is cost effective. For example, a message that costs $3.12 when sent by telephone, or $1.46 by fax, costs only 23 cents by e-mail. In addition to cost savings, there is a speed advantage. Messages can be transferred between countries in minutes and within the United States in seconds. On the other hand, network outages, maintenance, or repair problems may cause a message to be delayed days or even weeks. As e-mail continues to gain in popularity, the U.S. Postal Service and telephone services may find their market share declining.

> Between 1988 and 1994, the U.S. Postal Service's market share dropped from 77 to 62 percent, while electronic alternatives increased their share from 19 to 36 percent.

Setting Up Messenger

You will use the Messenger component of Netscape Communicator to create and send your e-mail message.

> The menu equivalent is **C**ommunicator/ **M**essenger Mailbox, and the keyboard shortcut is Ctrl + 2.

- Start Netscape Communicator and, if necessary, enter your user ID and password to gain access to the Internet.

- Click ▢▢ Mailbox from the Component bar.

Your screen should be similar to Figure 3-1.

FIGURE 3-1

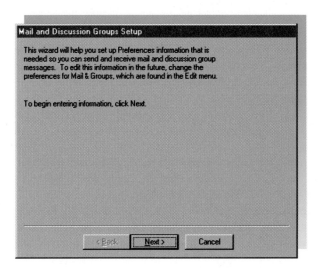

The Mail and Discussion Groups Setup Wizard is displayed by default when you first use Messenger. A wizard is a series of dialog boxes that guide you through the completion of a procedure. In this case, the wizard will help you set up or configure Messenger so that it knows the address of your Internet server, and your name and e-mail address. Without this information, Messenger does not know how to route or store your messages. To use the wizard to enter your preferences,

> If your setup does not display the wizard, your instructor will provide you with the instructions for setting preferences manually.

- ■ Click Next > .
- ■ In the Your Name text box enter your real name.

The second item you need to enter is your e-mail address.

Concept 2: E-Mail Address

On the Internet, each person has a unique e-mail address or means of identification. The Internet uses an addressing system called the **Domain Name System (DNS)**, which consists of three parts: a unique user name, a domain name and a domain code, as shown below.

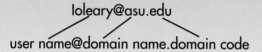

loleary@asu.edu

user name@domain name.domain code

The user name identifies a particular user or group of users at a domain. It is separated from the domain name with the @ ("at") symbol. The domain name distinguishes a computer from a group of computers. The domain code identifies the type of use. The most common domains are commercial organizations or educational and research institutions. The domain code is generally a three-letter abbreviation; for example, edu for education and com for commercial. Periods, called dots, separate the domain name and code. The number of dots varies depending on how the address is structured for a particular computer.

- ■ Enter your complete e-mail address in the Email Address text box.

> E-mail addresses are not case sensitive.

Your screen should be similar to Figure 3-2.

FIGURE 3-2

```
┌─────────────────────────────────────────────┐
│ Mail and Discussion Groups Setup            │
│                                              │
│  The information below is needed before you can send mail. If you do not │
│  know the information requested, please contact your system administrator │
│  or Internet Service Provider.               │
│                                              │
│  Your name:                                  │
│  ┌──────────────────────┐                    │
│  │ Student Name         │ (e.g. John Smith)  │
│  └──────────────────────┘                    │
│                                              │
│  Email address:                              │
│  ┌──────────────────────┐                    │
│  │ Yourusername@asu.edu │ (e.g. jsmith@company.com) │
│  └──────────────────────┘                    │
│                                              │
│  Outgoing mail [SMTP] server:                │
│  ┌──────────────────────┐                    │
│  │ smtp.asu.edu         │                    │
│  └──────────────────────┘                    │
│                                              │
│  You do not have to enter this information now. Click next to continue. │
│                                              │
│      < Back     Next >     Cancel            │
└─────────────────────────────────────────────┘
```

Next you need to identify your mail servers.

Concept 3: Mail Servers

Two mail servers work together to handle incoming and outgoing e-mail messages. The outgoing mail server uses the **Simple Mail Transport Protocol (SMTP)** to send messages over the Internet. The incoming mail server commonly uses either the **Internet Message Access Protocol (IMAP)** or the **Post Office Protocol (POP)** to deliver messages to your mailbox. Both have different advantages and disadvantages.

IMAP keeps messages individually in your mailbox on your incoming mail server. When you receive your mail, the address and subject lines only are downloaded to your computer. Then when you select a message to read, its content is downloaded. When you make changes to your messages, such as deleting messages, these changes are copied back from your computer to your mailbox on the incoming mail server. Therefore you always have access to an updated mailbox. The disadvantage to this system is if your connection to your server goes down while you are reading e-mail. Then only the content of the current message is on your local computer and you must reestablish a connection before you can read more messages. Additionally, connect time is usually longer because you must either be connected to the mail server while you are reading your messages, or you must reconnect every time you access a message you haven't read.

POP copies entire e-mail messages to your computer all at once after you connect to the mail server. Therefore, if you lose your connection, you still have all your messages. The major disadvantage is that when you make changes to messages stored in your computer mailbox you must also make the same changes to the messages on your mail server's mailbox. If you do not synchronize both mailboxes, it can result in downloading new messages over and over (if you save your messages on your server) each time you connect, or can result in messages residing on computers you have previously used but to which you may not currently have access. The end result is you are sometimes unable to access all your messages when you need to.

> If you are using a school computer, the mail server settings may already be entered correctly in the dialog box.

In the Outgoing Mail Server text box, you tell Messenger where to find the mail that has been sent to you.

- Enter the SMTP information in the text box as indicated by your instructor.

- Click [Next >].

In the next dialog box you specify the incoming mail server settings (see Figure 3-3). The mail server user name is your user name (the first part of your e-mail address).

- Enter your mail server user name in the appropriate text box.

- Enter the outgoing mail server and incoming mail server information as provided by your instructor.

- If necessary, select the appropriate mail server type as indicated by your instructor.

Your screen should be similar to Figure 3-3.

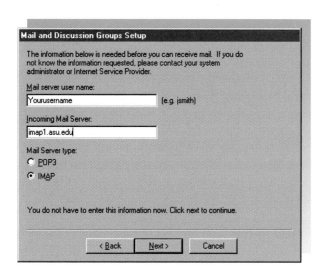

FIGURE 3-3

Your instructor will inform you of any other settings that need to be changed.

The last wizard box is used to set the discussion group server that you will use in Lab 4.

■ Click   Next >   .

■ If necessary, enter the NNTP server information provided by your instructor.

■ Click   Finish   .

The wizard is closed and the required settings to use Messenger are established. Your screen should be similar to Figure 3-4.

The NNTP server is the computer that handles newsgroup messages. You will learn about this feature in Lab 4.

If necessary, enter the password for your account.

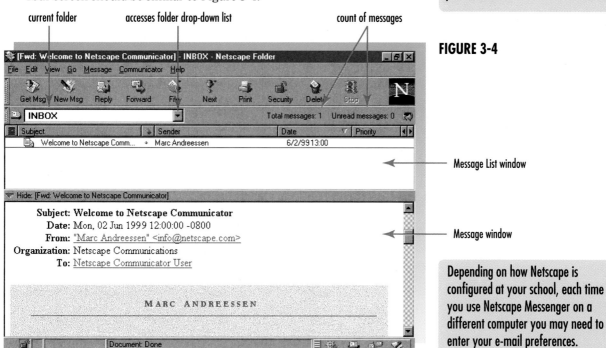

current folder   accesses folder drop-down list   count of messages

FIGURE 3-4

Message List window

Message window

Depending on how Netscape is configured at your school, each time you use Netscape Messenger on a different computer you may need to enter your e-mail preferences.

The Messenger window is divided into two panes. The upper pane displays the Message List window. It contains message header summaries that help identify each message. The three items of information in the message header are the subject of the message, the name and/or e-mail address of the sender, and the date and time the message was received.

The lower pane contains the Message window in which the text for the selected (highlighted) message is displayed. When you first use Netscape to access your mail account, you may receive an e-mail message welcoming you to Netscape similar to that shown in Figure 3-4. Otherwise, if you have not used your mail account before, your Message window may be empty.

In addition, the window contains menus and toolbar buttons that are used to create and manage e-mail messages. The Location toolbar contains a folder drop-down list box that displays the name of the mail folder you are accessing.

Concept 4: Folder

A **folder** is an area on your disk that is used to organize and store messages. The following folders are included with Messenger.

Folder	Stores
Inbox	Incoming messages
Unsent	Messages that were not sent
Drafts	Messages that you are still working on
Sent	Messages that were sent
Trash	Messages that have been deleted

You can also create your own folders to store different categories of messages. To move messages into a different folder, select the message header, then click [ ] and select the folder you want to move it to. Even easier is to drag the message header from the message list to the [ ] button and drop it into a folder in the folder list.

Organizing your messages can save you a lot of time when you are looking for a message sent or received some time ago. To help you locate messages, you can use the Search command in the Edit menu. It allows you to enter a keyword to search on and to specify which parts of messages you want to search as well as which folder.

> The Inbox folder is open by default whenever you open Messenger.

The right side of the location toolbar shows a count of the total number of messages in the folder and the number that have not been read.

Composing a Message

To create a new e-mail message,

■ Click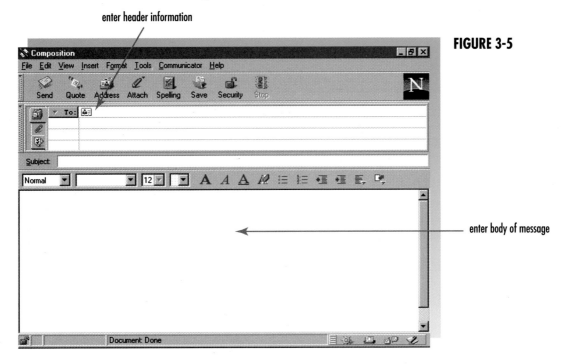

The menu equivalent is **M**essage/**N**ew Message, and the keyboard shortcut is (Ctrl) + M.

■ Maximize the Composition window.

Your screen should be similar to Figure 3-5.

enter header information

FIGURE 3-5

enter body of message

The Composition window is used to write, edit, and send e-mail messages. The buttons below the title bar are shortcuts for menu options commonly used while creating a message. The upper section of the window contains the area where you enter the header information, and the lower section is where you enter the text for the body of your message.

Concept 5: Parts of an E-Mail Message

An e-mail message consists of two basic parts, the header and the body. The header consists of the lines at the top of the message that tell the computer where to send the message. It is similar to the format used in a standard memo. The body is the large blank area in the center of the screen where you type your message content. Most e-mail programs include basic word processing features to help you create and edit your message.

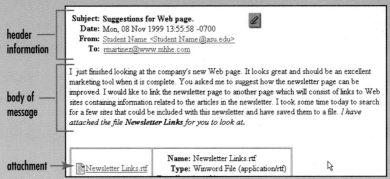

Typically the header consists of five lines: Subject, Date, From, To, and CC. In addition, many headers include a line for attachments. These lines are described below.

Subject: A brief description of the contents of the message. Although not required by Messenger, it is very helpful when you receive messages in reminding you of the content of the message.

Date: The current date is displayed on this line and identifies the date the message was sent.

From: Contains the e-mail address of the sender of the message. This information is automatically entered for you.

To: Contains the e-mail address of the recipient of the message. There are six different recipient types:

To	Primary recipient of your message.
CC	Carbon Copy—for secondary recipients.
BCC	Blind Carbon Copy—for secondary recipients not identified to the other recipients, including those in the BCC list.
Group	Posting to a discussion group.
Reply-To	Response to the sender of a message.
Followup-To	A follow-up response to message.

Attachment: A text or non-text file, such as graphic file, spreadsheet, or Web page, that is sent along with your e-mail message. The attached file is downloaded to the recipient's computer where it can be opened using the specific software program.

In addition, one feature many people like to add to their e-mail messages is a **signature line** that is automatically added to the end of a message, much like a closing in a letter. Generally, the signature line includes the sender's full name, postal address, phone number, fax number, and other e-mail addresses. Additionally, the signature may include a quote or some other "signature" that is a means of showing a bit of your personality. You can add a signature line by using **E**dit/Pr**e**ferences/Mail & Groups/Identity.

The first item you will specify in the header is the recipient. Every message must include this addressing information so the program knows where to send the message. You can enter an e-mail address, a nickname, a mailing-list name, or the name of a discussion group as the recipient. Most commonly, an e-mail address is entered.

To see the different recipient types,

■ Click ▾ To:.

The drop-down list displays the different addressing types. You can also select multiple delivery recipients for a single message.

You want to send an e-mail message to your supervisor, Ramon Martinez, at The Sports Company. Since you want to send the message to an individual, you will use the default To recipient type. To close the drop-down list and enter your supervisor's e-mail address in the To line,

■ Click [⚏=].

■ Type **rmartinez@www.mhhe.com**

■ Press Tab ⇥.

You are now ready to enter the subject for the message. The subject should be brief (many mailers will truncate long subject lines) and yet descriptive of the contents of the message. As much of the subject line as space allows will be displayed on the recipient's incoming message header. A subject line that pertains clearly to the e-mail body is a good way to get people in the right context to receive your message. To enter a subject for your message,

■ Type **Suggestions for Web page**

■ Click in the message area.

Your screen should be similar to Figure 3-6.

You will learn about nicknames later in this lab, and about mailing lists and discussion groups in Lab 4.

The **E**dit/Search Director**y** command will access Web directories from which you can conduct a search for a person's e-mail address. Refer to Lab 2 Finding People and Businesses to learn about these features.

If the recipient is on the same local area network as you, such as your school or business, you can shorten the e-mail address to the user name only.

You could also press Esc or click in a blank area to cancel the drop-down list.

If you press ←Enter you will create another address line instead of moving to the Subject line. To remove the extra line, press Backspace.

insertion point   e-mail address   subject line

FIGURE 3-6

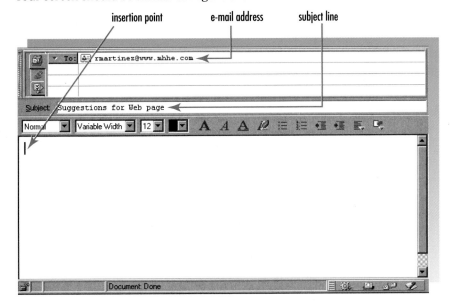

The insertion point appears at the left margin of the first line where you can begin to type your message.

Because of its speed and fast turnaround time, e-mail is fundamentally different from paper-based communication. In a paper document, it is absolutely essential to make everything completely clear and unambiguous because your audience may not have a chance to ask for clarification. With e-mail documents, your recipient can ask questions immediately. E-mail style thus tends, like conversational speech, to be much sloppier and more ambiguous. In addition, e-mail has developed its own set of guidelines for courteous communication, called Netiquette.

Concept 6: E-Mail Style and Netiquette

E-mail is a fairly new way of communicating and has developed its own style and set of rules of courteous electronic communications called **Netiquette** (net etiquette). As a new user you might be unaware of the meanings and subtleties of e-mail communication. The following are some e-mail style guidelines.

- When corresponding in a work or business situation, be careful what you write and how you write it. Spelling, grammar, and so on may not seem important at the time, but later you may regret any informality.

- In informal communications to friends and family, many people use special pictures of smiling or winking faces called **smileys** or **emoticons** to communicate feelings. They are created using combinations of characters, such as a colon, hyphen, and right parenthesis to create a happy smiley.

Smiley	Meaning
:-)	Happy
:-(	Sad
;-)	Wink
:-P	Sticking tongue out
:-||	Angry
:-o	Shocked or amazed

Smileys are generally placed following the sentence in question. Other e-mail users enclose remarks in brackets such as <g> for "grin" and <jk> for "just kidding."

■ In addition, in informal communications, many people use abbreviations for commonly used phrases to save typing time. Some examples are shown below.

Abbreviation	Meaning
ASAP	As soon as possible
FYI	For your information
PLS	Please
THX	Thanks
BTW	By the way
BCNU	Be seeing you
FWIW	For what it's worth
F2F	Face to face
IMHO	In my humble opinion
IRL	In real life
OBO	Or best offer
LOL	Laughing out loud
ROTFL	Rolling on the floor laughing
TNSTAAFL	There's no such thing as a free lunch
TTFN	Ta ta for now
TTYL	Talk to you later

It is easy to become too informal when using e-mail. It is still written communication, and like all written communication, the messages can be saved and printed. You can then be made accountable for your words.

The following are some Netiquette guidelines.

■ Be concise. One of the many benefits of e-mail is its ability to answer a question or communicate a thought more quickly than a letter. Keeping e-mails short and to the point helps keep the recipient's attention and makes e-mail more productive.

■ DO NOT TYPE YOUR MESSAGES IN ALL UPPERCASE CHARACTERS! This is called **shouting** and is perceived to be very offensive. Use a normal combination of uppercase and lowercase characters. Sometimes all lowercase is perceived as too informal or timid.

■ If your e-mail program does not automatically word wrap, keep line length to 60 characters or less so your messages can be comfortably displayed on any type of monitor.

■ Never send abusive, threatening, harassing, or bigoted messages. You could be held criminally liable for what you write.

■ Think twice before sending your message: generally, once it is sent, you cannot get it back.

Messenger contains a built-in text editor that helps you easily enter and edit your messages. Like a word processor, it automatically wraps the text to the beginning of the next line when the text reaches the right edge of the screen. Therefore, you do not need to press ⏎Enter at the end of each line. Press ⏎Enter only when you need to end a line or to insert a blank line.

As in other Windows-based applications, the mouse, scroll bars, and directional arrow keys can be used to move through the message area.

Mouse	Action
Click new location	Positions insertion point.
Click scroll arrow	Scrolls line by line or character by character in direction of scroll arrow.
Click above/below scroll box	Scrolls document window by window.
Drag scroll box	Moves multiple windows up/down.

Key	Action
→	One character to right
←	One character to left
↑	One line up
↓	One line down
Ctrl + →	One word to right
Ctrl + ←	One word to left
Home	Beginning of line
End	End of line
Page Up	Previous full window of text
Page Down	Next full window of text
Ctrl + Home	Beginning of message
Ctrl + End	End of message

To enter the message (type it exactly, including errors, as shown here),

■ Type **I have just finnished looking at the company's new Web page. It looks great and should be an excellent marketing tool when it is complete. You asked me to suggest how the newsletter page can be imporved. I would like to link the newsletter to another page, which will consist of links to Web sites containing information related to the articles in the newsletter. I took some time today to search for a few sites that could be included with this newsletter and have saved them to a file. I have attached the file Newsletter Links for you to look at.**

This message contains intentional typing errors. Do not be concerned if you make additional errors, you will learn how to correct them shortly.

Your screen should be similar to Figure 3-7.

FIGURE 3-7

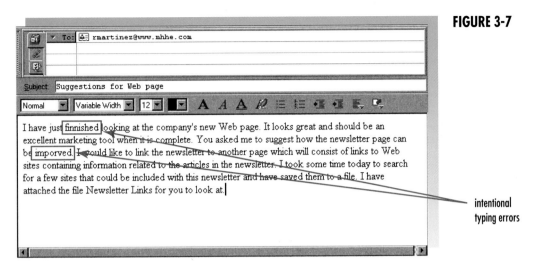

intentional
typing errors

Checking Spelling

To ensure that your message does not contain spelling or typing errors, most e-mail programs include a spell-checking feature. To locate errors, the program checks each word in the message against a dictionary of words. If it cannot find a match, it highlights the word so you can edit it if needed. To spell-check this message,

■ Click [Spelling].

Your screen should be similar to Figure 3-8.

> The menu equivalent is **T**ools/Check
> **Spelling**.

misspelled word   starts spelling checker   suggested replacement

FIGURE 3-8

option buttons

misspelled word identified
with a red dashed underline

The Check Spelling dialog box is displayed and the located misspelled word "finnished" is highlighted in the message. Notice that the misspelled words are also displayed with red dashed lines under them. The Suggestions list box displays the words in the program's dictionary that most closely match the misspelled word. The first word is highlighted. Sometimes the Check Spelling feature does not display any suggested replacements because it cannot locate any words that are similar in spelling in the dictionary.

To tell the Check Spelling feature what to do, you need to choose from the following six options:

Option	Effect
Replace	Changes word to the selected word in the Suggestions box.
Replace All	Replaces word throughout the document with the word in the Suggestions box.
Check	Verifies the entry in the Word text box using the dictionary.
Ignore	Accepts word as correct for this occurrence only.
Ignore All	Accepts word as correct throughout the spell checking of the document.
Learn	Adds the entry in the Word text box to the dictionary and replaces the selected word. If there are several entries in the Word text box, each one is added to the dictionary.

To change the spelling of the word to one of the suggested spellings, highlight the correct word in the list and then choose ▭ Replace ▭. Because "finished" is already highlighted and is the correct replacement,

■ Click ▭ Replace ▭

If there were no suggested replacements, and you did not want to use any of the option buttons, you could edit the word yourself by typing the correction in the Word text box.

Your screen should be similar to Figure 3-9.

corrected word

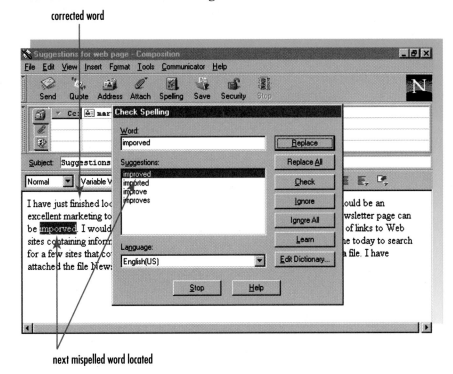

FIGURE 3-9

next misspelled word located

The spell checker replaces the misspelled word in the message with the correct spelling and continues to check the message for other errors.

■   Correct the spelling of any other words the program locates.

■   Click [Done].

> When no more errors are located, the [Replace] button changes to [Done].

Editing a Message

Before sending an e-mail message, you should reread it for accuracy and clarity. Having done this, you would like to edit your message by changing a few words. Some basic mouse and keyboard selecting and editing features are shown in the tables below.

To select:	Procedure:
word	Double-click in the word.
line	Click in the left margin next to the line.
multiple lines	Drag in the left margin bar next to the lines.
paragraph	Double-click in the left margin next to the paragraph.
multiple paragraphs	Drag in the left margin next to the paragraphs.
entire message	**E**dit/Select **A**ll or [Ctrl] + A

Editing Procedure	Shortcut Key	Effect
	Backspace	Deletes character to left of insertion point or current selection
	Delete	Deletes character to right of insertion point or current selection
Edit/**U**ndo	Ctrl + Z	Reverses last action or command
Edit/**R**edo	Ctrl + Y	Repeats last action or command
Edit/**C**ut	Ctrl + X	Removes selected text and places copy in Clipboard
Edit/**C**opy	Ctrl + C	Copies selected text to Clipboard
Edit/**P**aste	Ctrl + V	Pastes text from Clipboard

> Clipboard is a temporary storage area on your system.

■ Double-click the word "have" in the first sentence.

■ Press Delete.

■ Add the word "page" following the word "newsletter" in the fourth sentence.

■ Reread the message and use the editing features to correct any typing mistakes.

Formatting Your Message

To enhance the appearance of your message, you can add formatting to your text. For example, you can change the font style and size, add color, bold, underlines, and italics. You can also emphasize important text with bullets and/or numbered lists, change the alignment of text, and insert objects such as pictures into the message. These features are mostly in the Format menu or on the Formatting toolbar located above the message area. Documents that include such formatting enhancements are called **rich-text documents**.

> In order for recipients to view the enhancements, they must also have an e-mail program that supports rich-text formatting.

> The file extension .rtf identifies a file as a rich-text file.

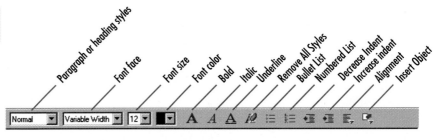

You would like to italicize the last sentence of the memo and bold the name of the file. To do this,

■ Select the last sentence.

■ Click [A] Italics.

> The menu equivalent is F**o**rmat/**S**tyle/**I**talic, and the keyboard shortcut is Ctrl + I.

- Select the words "Newsletter Links."

- Click ■ Bold.

- Click in the last sentence to clear the highlight.

The menu equivalent is F**o**rmat/**S**tyle/**B**old, and the keyboard shortcut is [Ctrl] + B.

Your screen should be similar to Figure 3-10.

Formatting toolbar

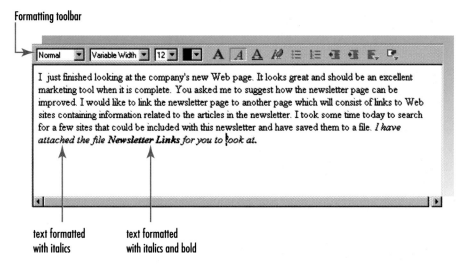

FIGURE 3-10

text formatted
with italics

text formatted
with italics and bold

The sentence is now displayed in italics and the file name is bold. You can add as many enhancements as you like to a message. But keep in mind that, as with any other type of document, too many enhancements can clutter a document and make it hard to read.

Attaching Files

The last thing you need to do before sending this message is to attach the file to the message. The ability to send files attached to your e-mail message is a very convenient feature. For example, if you are working on a group project you can e-mail your section of the project to another member of your group. This makes it easy to get information to each other without having to meet in person. You can attach files of any type, including text, sound, graphics, and Web pages. For the attachment to be read by recipients, they must have the appropriate software program.

You can send a Web page that you are viewing in an e-mail message using **F**ile/**Send** Page in Navigator. The Composition window is opened with the page embedded already. Just address and send.

- Click Attach.

- Choose **F**ile as the type of attachment.

The menu equivalent is **F**ile/A**tt**ach/**F**ile.

The Enter File to Attach dialog box on your screen should be similar to Figure 3-11.

FIGURE 3-11

specify location of file

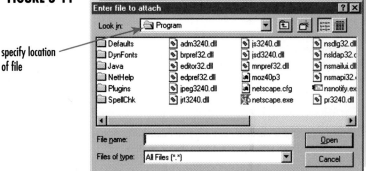

From this dialog box you identify the file you want to attach. This is similar to the File Open dialog box you have used in other applications to open a document. You will attach the text file you created in Lab 2 and saved on your data disk.

If the Newsletter Links file is not available, use the Related Links.rtf file on your data disk.

■ From the Look In drop-down list, select the drive that contains your data disk.

■ Select Newsletter Links.rtf.

■ Click **Open** .

Your screen should be similar to Figure 3-12.

includes an attachment with message

attachment reference

FIGURE 3-12

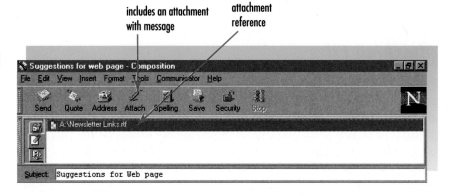

Notice that the file name you just selected, along with its path, is displayed in the Attachment tab of the message header. When you send this message, a copy of the file will be sent along with the message.

Sending a Message

Now that your message is complete, you can send it.

■ Click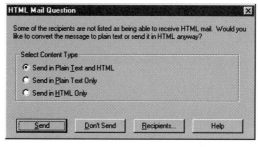

The HTML Mail Question dialog box may appear, asking you how you want the message sent. Messages can be sent as plain text documents or HTML documents. Plain text documents display the document text only without formatting, whereas HTML documents are rich-text documents that can display all formatting and graphics elements. If you are in

doubt as to what to do, plain-text only is the most efficient type of message to send. Because everyone at The Sports Company can read rich-text messages, you will send the message in HTML format.

■ If the HTML Mail Question dialog box is displayed, select Send in HTML Only.

■ Click Send .

The Sending Message box displays a progress bar showing the progress of the message as it is copied to the server.

How do you know the message was sent? Always assume that it was. If it is not sent, it is bounced back to you with a message from your mail administrator indicating the reason why. The most common reason is an incorrectly entered e-mail address.

progress bar

Opening an Attachment

The Composition window is closed, and the Message List window is displayed again. When Netscape sends a message, it automatically keeps a copy of the message for you in the Sent folder.

To verify that your message was saved,

■ Select Sent from the folder drop-down list box.

> If the message content is not displayed, choose **V**iew/Show Message.

The upper pane of the window displays a message header summary.

■ If necessary, scroll the message header pane to display the message header of the message you sent.

■ Click on the Suggestions for Web page message header.

Your screen should be similar to Figure 3-13.

scrolls message header information

Sent mail folder

message header summary

displays message selected in upper pane

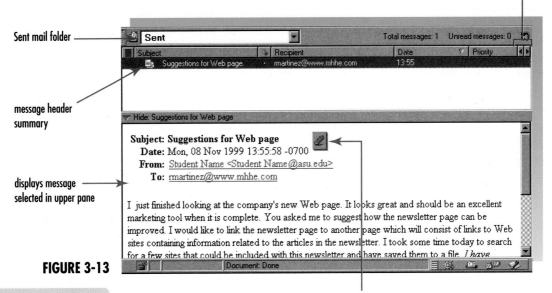

FIGURE 3-13

indicates message includes an attachment

> If only a time is displayed, the current date is assumed.

> Additional header information such as the message priority, status, and size can be displayed by clicking the scroll buttons ▣▣ at the right end of the message header bar.

> You can double-click the shortcut to open the attachment.

> If your e-mail programs are not compatible, the attachment may not be readable upon receipt.

> Your attachment link may appear as <u>Part 1.2</u>.

The content of the selected message is displayed in the message pane. The message appears exactly as it will appear when received by the regional manager. The ▨ symbol means the message includes an attachment. Clicking on the ▨ symbol displays a shortcut icon with the file name of the attachment.

■ Scroll the message pane to view the end of the message.

The attachment box includes a link to the file and information that includes the name of the

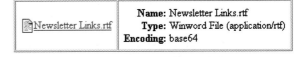

file and file type. To open an attachment, you click on the link. If Netscape recognizes the file format (identified by the file extension), it will open the application and display the file. If it does not recognize the file type, you must save the file and then open it using the correct software program.

■ Click <u>Newsletter Links.rtf</u>.

When you open attached files, a warning dialog box is displayed advising you that opening this file could start a computer virus that may have detrimental effects on your system. This is one of the hazards of e-mail. Open only attachments whose source you trust. Protect your computer by using a virus-checker program to check the attachment before opening it on your computer. Then, if you are unsure of an attachment, save it to your disk rather than open it so that the virus-checker program can check it first.

> Some e-mail messages you receive may warn you that an e-mail message carries a virus. Simply reading the message cannot trigger the virus. Only e-mail attachments can carry a virus.

- ■ Select **O**pen it.

- ■ Click [OK].

- ■ If necessary, maximize the word processor window.

Your screen should be similar to Figure 3-14.

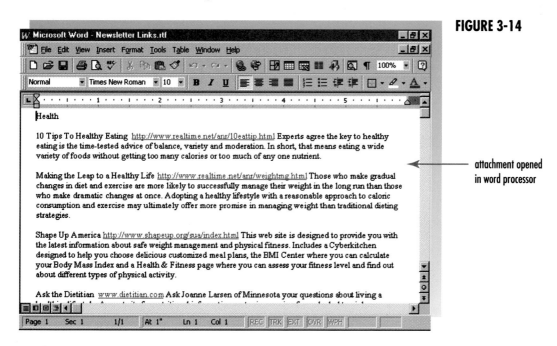

FIGURE 3-14

attachment opened in word processor

Because Netscape recognizes this file as a rich-text file from the file extension .rtf, the word processor on your system is automatically loaded and the file of Web site descriptions is displayed.

- ■ Click 🗙 to close the file and exit the word processor.

Checking Incoming Mail

After checking your message, you decide to see if you have received any new mail. When you load Netscape Messenger it automatically checks for incoming mail. By default, Netscape checks for new mail every ten minutes. If new mail

The menu equivalent is **F**ile/**G**et Messages/**N**ew, and the keyboard shortcut is Ctrl + T.

has been received, the mail icon in the component bar displays a green dot. You can also check for mail manually by clicking ![Get Msg] at any time.

■   Open the Inbox folder.

■   Click ![Get Msg].

If the No Messages on Server message box is displayed, click OK. Wait a few minutes and try again.

The Getting New Messages box advises you of the number of new messages waiting to be delivered and the progress of the delivery as the messages are downloaded to your computer.

Your screen should be similar to Figure 3-15.

indicates descending date order

FIGURE 3-15

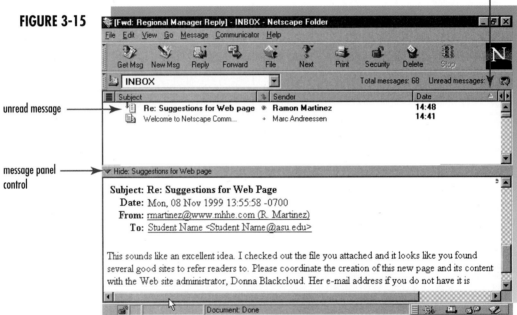

unread message

message panel control

The Inbox can display messages in ascending or descending date order. The triangle symbol in the Date button of the message header points up to indicate descending order and down to indicate ascending order. You want to display the most recently received messages at the top of the list.

You can change the category on which the messages are sorted using the **V**iew/**S**ort command.

■   If necessary, click the Date column header to change the date order to descending.

The menu equivalent is **V**iew/**S**ort/by Dat**e**/**D**escending.

A reply message from the regional manager should be displayed at the top of the message header list. The information in the Inbox message header is essentially the same as in the Sent folder except that the sender's rather than the recipient's name or e-mail address is displayed, and the date is the date received. Reading messages in the Inbox folder is the same as in the Sent folder.

Notice that the mail icon to the left of the Subject is an open letter ![open]. This indicates the message has been read. This icon appears as a closed letter ![closed] when the message has not been read.

Many times when there are many new messages, you may want to see more message headers so you can selectively read them. To do this you can minimize the message pane.

■   Click ![arrow] (message panel control).

Your screen should be similar to Figure 3-16.

FIGURE 3-16

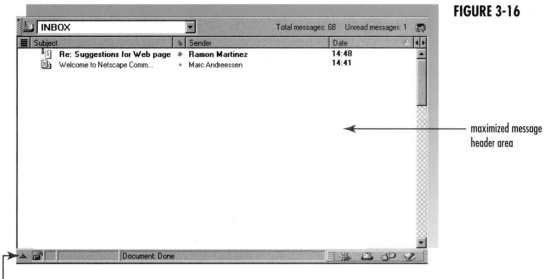

maximized message
header area

message panel control

The message pane is minimized. Now the message panel control icon appears in the status bar. To display the message pane again,

■   Click ▲.

> The menu equivalent is **V**iew/Hide Message or Show Message.

You can also adjust the size of the message pane to display more or less of the message header window by dragging the divider between panes downward. If you drag too far down, the message pane is minimized.

If the message is long you can use the scroll bar to read, it or you can double-click on the message header to display the message in a separate message window. Then you do not have to scroll as often to read the message.

■   Double-click the Re: Suggestions for Web page message header.

■   If necessary, maximize the window.

> The menu equivalent is **F**ile/**O**pen Message.

Your screen should be similar to Figure 3-17.

FIGURE 3-17

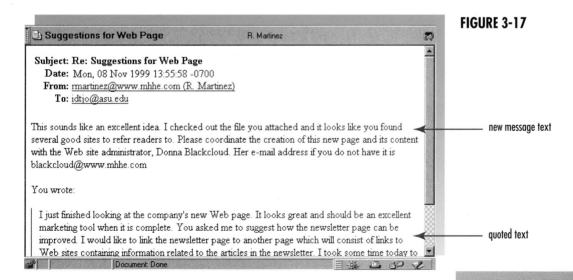

new message text

quoted text

The appearance of a reply varies with the e-mail program used. Quoted text is commonly preceded with the > symbol and appears in italics.

Notice that the regional manager has included the full content of your message in his reply to you. This is called **quoting** and provides the recipient with a frame of reference as to the message that is being responded to. The new text of the message appears above the quote.

Creating an Address Book

The regional manager's reply includes the e-mail address for Donna Blackcloud, the Web administrator for The Sports Company site. You need to contact this person about the new page and make plans on how to proceed. Since you will probably be working closely with this person, you decide to add the e-mail address to your address book.

Concept 7: Address Book

Rather than trying to remember many different e-mail addresses, you can create a file of addresses called an **address book**. Then when you select a name from the address book, the e-mail address is automatically entered in the To header line. Using the address book is like speed-dialing a phone number, and like speed dialing it is faster and more accurate.

Entries in the address book include the person's full name, a nickname, their e-mail address, organization, and title. A **nickname** is an easy-to-remember shortcut for a person's e-mail address. It can be entered in the To header line and Messenger will replace it with the e-mail address when the message is sent. This is helpful when you send a lot of mail to the same person. You can also specify with each address whether they can receive plain-text only or rich-text (HTML) formatted messages. When this information is included in the address book, the message is automatically sent to that person in the specified format, and the HTML Mail Question dialog box is not displayed.

In addition, you can create a mailing list consisting of a list of names in the address book. The list is assigned a name that is added to the address book as an alias. Then by entering the mailing list name in the To header line, you can quickly send the same message to all the people on the list.

The address book can also be used to store other contact information such as postal addresses and phone numbers.

Unlike other address book entries, the mailing list does not have an e-mail address of its own.

Usually you add an address to the address book by typing it in directly or by copying it from the message header of a message you received. In this case, because the address is included in the message you are viewing, you will copy it from the message to the address book.

The keyboard shortcut is Ctrl + ⇧Shift + 2.

- ■ Select the e-mail address for Donna Blackcloud and choose Edit/Copy to copy it to the Clipboard.

- ■ Choose Communicator/Address Book.

- ■ Click [New Card].

The New Card dialog box on your screen should be similar to Figure 3-18.

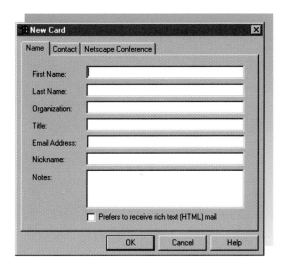

FIGURE 3-18

In the Name tab of this dialog box you enter the individual's personal information.

The Contact tab is used to enter additional information such as address and phone numbers.

- Click in the Email Address text box and press [Ctrl] + V (the Paste shortcut) to enter the e-mail address.

- Complete the remaining text boxes using the information shown below.

    First Name   **Donna**

    Last Name   **Blackcloud**

    Organization   **Southwest Regional office**

    Title   **Web Administrator**

    Nickname   **donna**

- Select Prefers to receive rich-text (HTML) mail.

- Click OK.

Your screen should be similar to Figure 3-19.

FIGURE 3-19

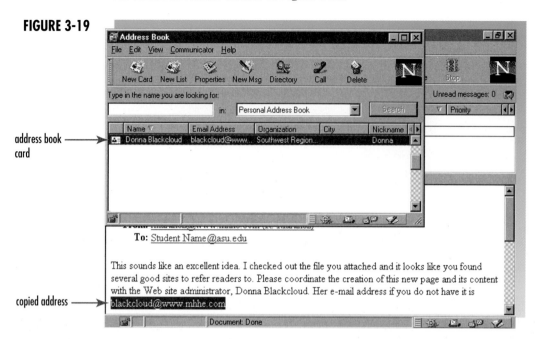

address book card

copied address

The new address entry is added to the address book. If there are multiple entries, they appear in alphabetical order. Next you will add the regional manager's address to the book. Another way to add an address is to copy the To header information from a message you have received.

> Delete address book entries by selecting the address entry and clicking Delete.

- Switch to the mail message window.
- Right-click on the message content area.
- Select Add to Address Book/Sender.

> The menu equivalent is **M**essage/**A**dd to Address Book/**S**ender.

A new address card is displayed with the sender's e-mail address automatically completed for you.

- Complete the remaining text boxes using the information shown below.

  First Name   **Ramon**

  Last Name   **Martinez**

  Organization   **Southwest Regional office**

  Title   **Regional Manager**

  Nickname   **Manager**

- Select Prefers to receive rich-text (HTML) mail.
- Click [OK].

> Your instructor will supply the necessary information.

- Finally, create a new address card that contains your instructor's e-mail address and information.
- Close the Address Book window.

Replying to E-Mail

When you are finished reading a message, you can either reply to it, forward it, file it, delete it, or just leave it. Many times after reading a message, you will want to reply to the message. When the message header is highlighted or you are viewing the message, it is not necessary to type in the recipient's address and subject information. The Reply command will automatically enter the sender's address as the recipient for you.

To reply to the message from Mr. Martinez (you should be viewing it),

- Click [Reply].
- Choose **R**eply to Sender.
- Maximize the window.

> The menu equivalent is **M**essage/**R**eply, and the keyboard shortcut in [Ctrl] + R.

Your screen should be similar to Figure 3-20.

indicates a reply   address of reply recipient automatically entered

FIGURE 3-20

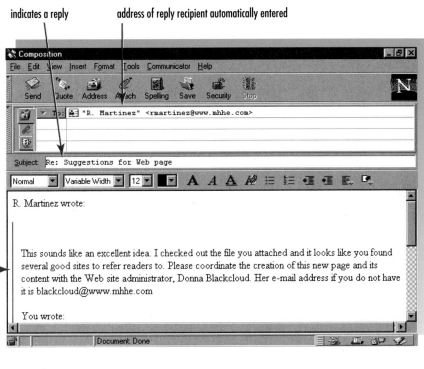

indicates quoted text

The address of the recipient automatically appears in the To text line, and the original subject text is entered following Re: in the Subject line. Netscape automatically quotes the entire original message by copying it into the body of the reply. The quoted text is preceded with a blue line in the left margin. If the original message is long and you are replying to only part of the message, edit the quoted text to include just enough to provide a context for the message and no more. Then add your own new message to the reply, just as you did when composing a new message.

> Quoting is the default setting when replying to a message. You can turn off this feature using **E**dit/Pr**e**ferences/ Mail & Groups/Messages.

If the content of the quoted message is important to the answer, put your new text below the quoted text; otherwise place any new text above the original message. To add your reply to the beginning of the message,

- Type **I will contact Donna Blackcloud today. The new Web page should be ready by the end of next week**.

- Press ⏎ twice.

- Proofread and spell-check the message.

- Click [Send].

- Close the message window.

The Messenger window with the Inbox folder open should be displayed again.

Forwarding a Message

Next you want to send Donna a copy of the original message you sent to the regional manager. Another convenient feature of e-mail is the ability to **forward** a message to another person. All that is needed when forwarding a message is to specify the address of the new recipient. The e-mail program automatically includes the text of the message you are forwarding. This saves retyping the same information. You will use the address you entered in your personal address book to forward the message to Donna.

> The menu equivalent is **M**essage/ Forwar**d** and the keyboard shortcut is Ctrl + L.

- Open the Sent folder.

- Select the message header line of the reply message you just sent to the regional manager.

- Click [Forward].

Your screen should be similar to Figure 3-21.

Forward message window

FIGURE 3-21

subject line indicates it is —
a forwarded message

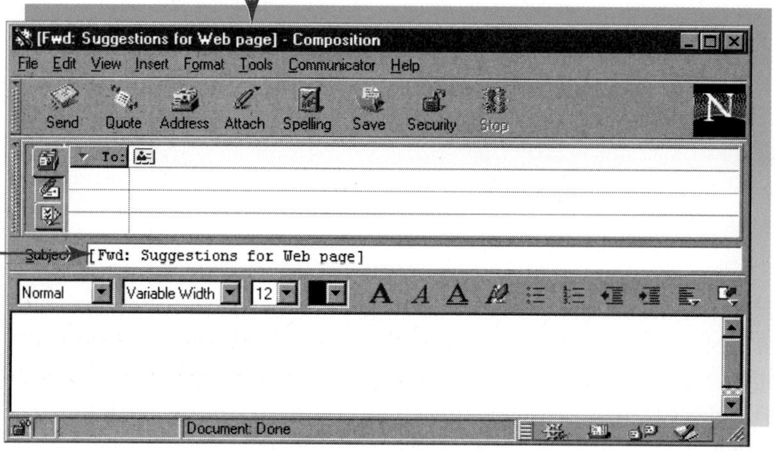

The subject line displays "FWD:" along with the original subject. Although the text area of the message appears blank, the original text is attached to the message and will be displayed when the message is received. The To line is blank so you can enter the address of the person you want to forward the message to. You will used Donna's nickname to enter her e-mail address from the address book in the To text line.

■ Type **do** in the To text box.

Notice that after typing the first few letters of the nickname, Netscape completes it for you automatically. You will also send a copy of this message to your instructor. To enter that e-mail address,

■ Click [Address].

■ Select your instructor's e-mail address.

■ Click [Cc:].

■ Click [OK].

The name of your instructor appears in the CC line. This is much faster than typing the entire address, and also minimizes errors when typing complicated e-mail addresses.

You can add text to the existing message, just as you would if composing a new message or replying to a message. To add a brief message of your own in the body above the forwarded message text, move to the message area.

■ Maximize the window.

■ Click in the message text area.

■ Type **I am forwarding a copy of a message I sent to Mr. Martinez about my suggestion for a new Web page on the company Web site. He has asked me to coordinate the creation of this page with you. Are you available any time tomorrow morning to discuss how to proceed?**

■ Proofread and spell check the message.

■ Send the message.

The message is forwarded to the recipient.

Saving a Message

Some messages you receive will contain information that you will want to keep or take with you to another location. You can save these messages in a folder you create or as a file on a disk. This is called **archiving**. You will save the message to your data disk.

■ Switch to the Inbox and select the message header of the reply you received from the regional manager.

■ Choose **F**ile/Save **A**s.

Do not delete the information in the subject line or the content of the forwarded message will not be sent. You can, however, add to the information line.

The menu equivalent is **F**ile/Selec**t** Addresses.

The keyboard shortcut is [Ctrl] + S.

The Save Messages As dialog box on your screen should be similar to Figure 3-22.

FIGURE 3-22

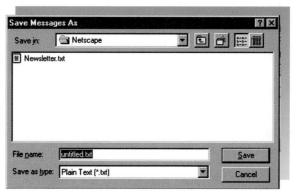

In this box you specify the location to save the file, the file name, and the file type. The default file type of plain text is correct. Using this format you can open the file using any word processing program.

■ Select the drive that contains your data disk from the Save In drop-down list.

■ Enter **Reply** as the file name.

■ Click [Save].

The file is saved on your data disk.

Deleting a Message

> Some mail servers limit the amount of disk space in your mailbox. If your mailbox is nearing capacity, you will receive a message advising you. You should then clean out your mailbox to make space for incoming mail.

Other messages, once read, are no longer needed. To clear your Inbox of unneeded mail, you can quickly delete messages. You will delete the message you just saved.

■ If necessary, select the message header of the reply you received from the regional manager.

■ Click [Delete].

> The Inbox Total Messages number has decreased by one.

Netscape removes the message from the Inbox and transfers it to the Trash folder. This is similar to Windows Recycle Bin. You can view messages in the Trash folder just like any other folder. If you want to restore a message that is in the Trash folder to the Inbox, you drag the file to the appropriate folder or use the File Message command on the Message menu. Not until you empty the Trash folder are the messages deleted from the disk.

> The menu equivalent is **Edit/Delete** Message.

■ Choose **File/Empty** Trash Folder to permanently delete the message.

■ If necessary, click [OK].

When you empty the Trash folder, Netscape automatically compacts the other folders to a size just large enough to hold the remaining mail.

Printing a Message

Finally, you will find there are many times that you will want to print a copy of a message. You will print the message you sent to Donna Blackcloud.

- ■ If necessary, prepare your printer to print.

- ■ Open the Sent folder.

- ■ Select the message header of the message to Donna Blackcloud.

- ■ Click ⏻ .

- ■ If necessary, select the appropriate printer for your system.

- ■ Click ⏻ OK ⏻ .

- ■ When you have completed this lab, exit Communicator and, if necessary, from the Internet.

> The menu equivalent is **File/Print** and the keyboard shortcut is Ctrl + P.

LAB REVIEW

■ ■ ■ ■ ■ ■ ■ ■ ■ ■ ■

Key Terms

address book   (NET98)
archive   (NET103)
Domain Name System (DNS)   (NET77)
e-mail   (NET75)
emoticon   (NET84)
folder   (NET80)
forward   (NET102)
Internet Message Access Protocol (IMAP)   (NET78)
mailbox   (NET75)
mailer program   (NET75)
mail server   (NET75)
Messenger   (NET75)
Netiquette   (NET84)
nickname   (NET98)
Post Office Protocol (POP)   (NET78)
quote   (NET98)
reader program   (NET75)
rich-text document   (NET90)
shout   (NET85)
signature line   (NET82)
Simple Mail Transport Protocol (SMTP)   (NET78)
smiley   (NET84)
store-and-forward   (NET75)

Command Summary

Command	Shortcut Key	Button	Action
Messenger Window			
File/**O**pen Message			Displays selected message in a separate message window
File/Ge**t** Messages/**N**ew	Ctrl + T	Get Msg	Gets new messages from server
File/Empt**y** Trash Folder			Permanently deletes messages
File/**P**rint		Print	Prints selected message
Edit/**U**ndo	Ctrl + Z		Reverses last action or command
Edit/**R**edo	Ctrl + Z		Repeats last action or command
Edit/Cu**t**	Ctrl + X		Cuts selected text to Clipboard
Edit/**C**opy	Ctrl + C		Copies selected text to Clipboard
Edit/**P**aste	Ctrl + V		Pastes text from Clipboard
Edit/**D**elete Message	Delete		Deletes selected message
Edit/**S**earch Directory			Accesses Web directories for a person's e-mail address
Edit/**P**references/Mail & Groups/Identity			Adds a signature line to e-mail messages
View/**H**ide Message		▼	Hides message content
View/**S**how Message		▲	Displays message content
View/S**o**rt			Changes order of display of e-mail messages
Message/**N**ew Message	Ctrl + M	New Msg	Creates a new e-mail message
Message/**R**eply	Ctrl + R	Reply	Creates a reply message to sender of selected message
Message/Forwar**d**	Ctrl + L	Forward	Forwards selected message to new address
Message/**A**dd to Address Book/**S**ender			Adds e-mail address of sender to address book
Communicator/**M**essenger Mailbox	Ctrl + 2		Opens Messenger component
Communicator/**A**ddress Book	Ctrl + ⇧ Shift + 2		Opens address book
Composition Window			
File/Sen**d** Now	Ctrl + ↵ Enter	Send	Sends a selected message to selected address
File/Send **L**ater			Stores e-mail to be sent at a different time
File/A**tt**ach/**F**ile		Attach	Adds an attachment to message
File/Selec**t** Addresses		Address	Selects addresses of recipients
Edit/Select **A**ll	Ctrl + A		Selects entire document
F**o**rmat/**S**tyle/**B**old	Ctrl + B	A	Bolds selected text
F**o**rmat/**S**tyle/**I**talics	Ctrl + I	A	Italicizes selected text
Tools/Check **S**pelling		Spelling	Starts the Spell-Checking feature

Matching

1. shouting   _____   **a.** electronic mail communications over a network

2. archive   _____   **b.** a happy emoticon

3. e-mail   _____   **c.** a text or non-text file that is attached to an e-mail message

4. header   _____   **d.** to send a message on to another recipient

5. doleary@mckenna.com   _____   **e.** rules of courteous e-mail communication

6. forward   _____   **f.** to save a message

7. :-)   _____   **g.** message entered in all uppercase letters

8. attachment   _____   **h.** addressing information of an e-mail message

9. Netiquette   _____   **i.** text of an e-mail message

10. body   _____   **j.** an e-mail address

Fill-In Questions

1. Using the sample e-mail message shown below, identify the parts by entering the correct term for each item.

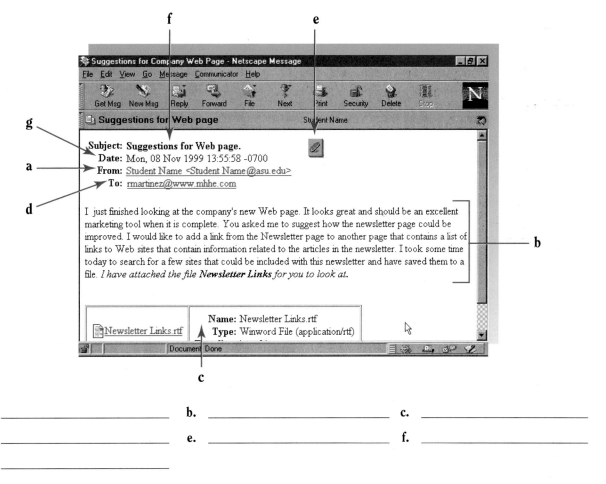

a. _____   b. _____   c. _____

d. _____   e. _____   f. _____

g. _____

Short-Answer Questions

1. What is e-mail? How is e-mail used?

2. What is store-and-forward technology?

3. What is the standard format of an e-mail address?

4. What is an attachment? How do you know if your message includes an attachment? How do you view an attachment?

5. What is a signature line?

6. What are the rules of courteous e-mail correspondence called? Discuss three rules and why they are important.

7. How can you express feelings when corresponding using e-mail? Give three examples.

8. Discuss several sources you can use to find an e-mail address.

9. Discuss the advantages of creating an e-mail address book or recipient list.

10. What are some problems associated with e-mail?

Hands-On Practice Exercises

Note: Your instructor will provide you with the To address for all practice problems.

Step by Step	Rating System		
	☆		Easy
	☆☆		Moderate
	☆☆☆		Difficult

1. Damon Lembi works for a computer training company. He has access to the Internet and needs information on when a new product is going to be available. He would like to send an e-mail message to his contact at a software supply company.

a. Start Netscape Messenger and compose the following new message:

To: <your user name@domain name>
Subject: Release of new product

Jack,

I am interested in finding out when you expect to receive the next upgrade of the word processing program I am currently using. I would like to begin preparing class materials so we are ready to go as soon as the product is available. Any help you may be able to provide is appreciated.

Thanks, <your name>

b. Carbon copy your instructor.

c. Spell-check the message and edit as needed.

d. Send the message.

e. Print a copy of the message you sent.

2. Joanne Clark uses e-mail to keep in contact with her outside sales representatives. She needs to send a message to two representatives that are attending a conference in another city.

Note: Your instructor will provide you with the To: e-mail address to complete this problem.

a. Compose the following message:

To: <user name@domain name>,
CC: <your user name@domain name>
Subject: New reporting procedure

Hope you are enjoying the conference.

I need to let you know that the company is implementing a new procedure for reporting sales orders. A new form has been designed to help us keep track of the increase in reorders by specific customers.

The new forms will be delivered to your hotel by FedEx this afternoon. If you have any questions about the new forms, send me a message and I will get back in touch with you.

Have fun and don't get too much sun.

Joanne Clark

b. Spell check the message and edit as needed.

c. Send the message.

Wait for the message to be placed in your mailbox. You would now like to reply to Joanne's message and ask her about the new forms.

d. Enter the following reply.

Joanne,

Do you want the orders that have not been submitted yet transferred to the new forms?

<your name>

e. Send the message. Print the message.

3. You would like to practice adding names to your address book.

a. Collect e-mail addresses from several friends, family, or classmates.

b. Add their names, e-mail addresses, and nicknames on new cards.

c. Select one of the names from the address book and compose a new message.

d. Before sending the message, you would like to carbon copy (CC) the message to your instructor. Use the address book to enter your instructor's address in the CC line.

e. Send the message.

f. Print a copy of the message you sent.

4. Your plan for the next issue of the Sports Company Update is to focus on health and fitness issues for children. You want to locate information on the WWW on this topic and provide a list of Web page descriptions to be included on the Related Links page for the next newsletter.

a. Start Netscape Communicator and search for information on health and fitness issues for children. Create a document in a word processor that contains the Web addresses and short descriptions of pages that would be appropriate for the newsletter.

b. Compose a new e-mail message addressed to Blackcloud@www.mhhe. Use the subject Next Quarter Newsletter Related Links. Include a CC to your instructor's e-mail address.

c. Enter the body of the message informing Donna Blackcloud about the next newsletter. Attach the word processor file of Web page descriptions. Send your message.

d. Print a copy of the message you sent.

On Your Own

5. Practice composing and sending messages by sending a message to a classmate. Have a classmate send a message to you. When you receive the message from your classmate, reply to it. Print the reply. Forward the message to another classmate.

6. In Lab 2 you learned how to search for e-mail addresses. If you have not already done so, complete Practice Exercise 3 in Lab 2. Use Four11 to locate your address or a friend's address. To create an address card directly from Four11, select the name and from the personal Web page choose Get vCard. Click the [Add to Address Book] button to open the address card. Complete any additional information. Close the address card, then click [Search These Results] to view the completed card. Click on the e-mail address and send a message to the address.

■ ■ ■ ■ ■ ■ ■ ■ □ □ □ □

Corresponding Using E-Mail

How E-Mail Works

E-mail requires the use of two programs: a mailer program and a delivery system.

E-Mail Address

On the Internet, each person has a unique e-mail address or means of identification.

Mail Servers

Two types of mail servers work together to handle incoming and outgoing e-mail messages.

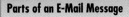

Parts of an E-Mail Message

An e-mail message consists of two basic parts, the header and the body.

E-Mail Style and Netiquette

E-mail is a fairly new way of communicating and has developed its own style and set of rules of courteous electronic communications called Netiquette (net etiquette).

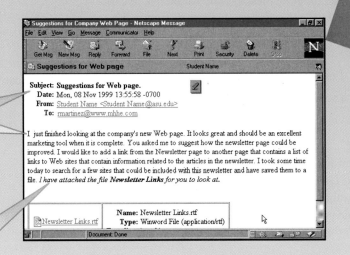

Concepts

How E-Mail Works
E-Mail Address
Mail Servers

Folder

Parts of an E-Mail Message
E-Mail Style and
  Netiquette

Address Book

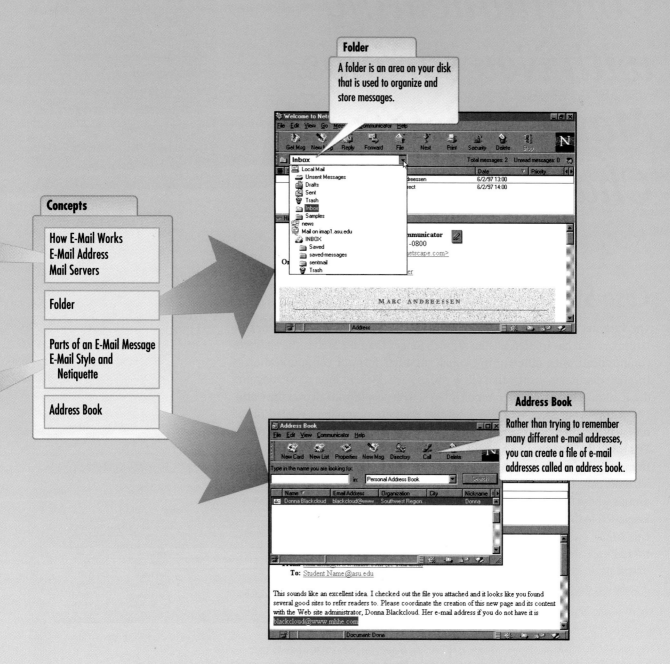

Folder

A folder is an area on your disk that is used to organize and store messages.

Address Book

Rather than trying to remember many different e-mail addresses, you can create a file of e-mail addresses called an address book.

Communicating with Newsgroups, Mailing Lists, and Chats

Case Study

The Internet consists of many parts in addition to the World Wide Web. One large part that has been in existence much longer than the Web is the ability to communicate with others using e-mail. Another form of communication is through discussion groups that allow you to participate in interactive, ongoing discussions about a topic of common interest with people from all over the world.

During your search for Web sites that contain information related to the newsletter content, you came across references and links to discussion groups. You think that it may also be useful to include links in the related topics links page to several discussion groups whose topic is related to information in the newsletter. You decide to use Netscape Communicator to locate and learn how to communicate in the different types of discussion groups.

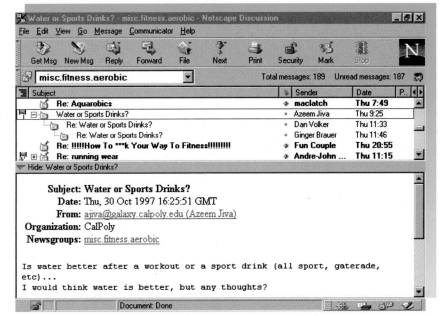

Concept Overview

The following concepts will be introduced in this lab:

1. Newsgroup

Newsgroups are special interest groups that are part of the network news system called Usenet, a network dedicated exclusively to the dissemination of newsgroup messages.

2. Categories of Newsgroups

Usenet organizes newsgroups into categories called hierarchies.

3. Thread

A thread is a newsgroup discussion about a specific topic with a common theme.

4. Newsgroup Culture

Newsgroups tend to develop personalities over time. The members get to know one another and think of their group as not just a location, but a place where they can talk with friends.

5. Mailing List

Mailing lists, also referred to simply as lists, consist of the e-mail addresses of a group of people who have subscribed to the mailing list because they are interested in the topic of the group.

6. Subscription Address and List Address

The subscription address is used to perform administrative tasks with the listserver, and the list address is used to communicate with mailing list members.

7. Chat Group

Communicating in a chat group means carrying on a conversation live (in real time) with other people over the Internet.

Starting Collabra

Discussion groups allow you to communicate with groups of people who have similar interests. They provide a great way to exchange ideas and information. They may not always offer accurate information, but they are generally a rich resource for learning about a topic. Three very popular types of discussion groups are mailing lists, newsgroups, and chat groups. Newsgroups and mailing lists rely on e-mail to exchange information, while chat groups allow direct "live" communication.

First you decide to look for newsgroups that may be discussing topics related to the articles in the newsletter.

Concept 1: Newsgroup

Newsgroups, also simply called groups, are special interest groups that are part of the network news system called **Usenet**, a network dedicated exclusively to the dissemination of newsgroup messages. Usenet distributes most, although not all, messages via the Internet. Newsgroup participants correspond using e-mail. However, unlike e-mail, messages are not sent to your personal inbox, instead they are sent to newsgroup sites for anyone to read. A **newsgroup site**, also called the **news server**, is a computer that participates in the Usenet network. Each site receives one copy of messages, called **articles**, which are sent or **posted** by the newsgroup members. The articles are stored on the site's disk, and after a period of time are removed. The length of time articles are stored is controlled by the news administrator at the site. The news administrator also decides what newsgroups to carry.

There are two types of newsgroups, moderated and unmoderated. In **moderated** newsgroups articles are sent to the moderator, who reviews or screens them for appropriateness before they are distributed. In **unmoderated** newsgroups the articles are not screened. Anyone can start an unmoderated newsgroup on any topic. Generally they consist of open and uncensored discussions.

Usenet is short for User's Network and is often spelled in all capital letters.

A large number of newsgroups are not part of Usenet. Their distribution is not as wide and they may not be carried by all Internet service providers.

It is estimated that there are more than 20,000 Usenet newsgroups, with new ones being added all the time (and others being removed).

To access newsgroups, you use a **newsreader program**. This program allows you to read newsgroup messages and presents them in an organized fashion. **Collabra** is the newsreader program included with Netscape Communicator.

■   Start Netscape Communicator.

■   Click 📧📰 Collabra Discussion groups.

■   If necessary, complete the Mail and Discussion Groups wizard as you did in Lab 3.

The menu equivalent is **C**ommunicator/ Collabra **D**iscussion Groups.

Your screen should be similar to Figure 4-1.

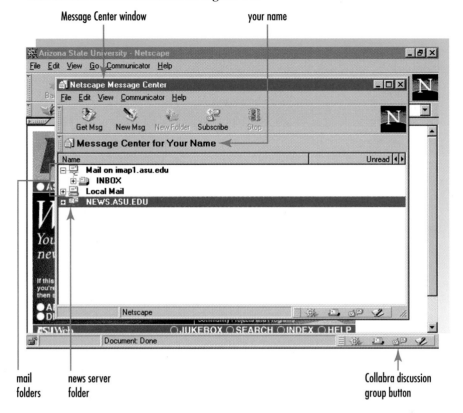

Message Center window   your name

FIGURE 4-1

mail folders   news server folder   Collabra discussion group button

Subscribing to Newsgroups

The Netscape Message Center displays your mail and news folders. When you first use Collabra, your news folder is empty. Your first step is to join or **subscribe** to the newsgroups you would be interested in reading. You must subscribe to newsgroups in order to participate in the discussion.

- ▪ If necessary, select the news server folder.

- ▪ Click [Subscribe].

> Your news server folder displays the name of the news server at your school.

> The menu equivalent is **F**ile/Su**b**scribe to Discussion Groups.

The Subscribe to Discussion Groups dialog box on your screen should be similar to Figure 4-2.

FIGURE 4-2

tabs ⟶

newsgroup ⟶
categories

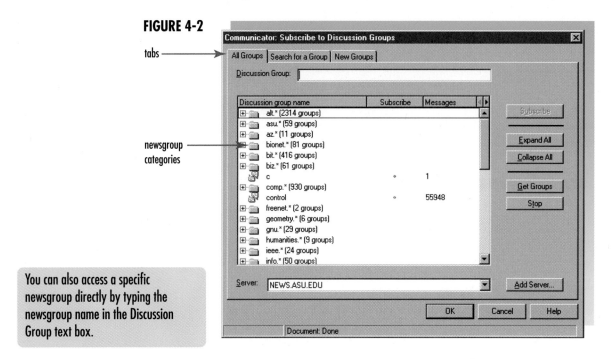

You can also access a specific newsgroup directly by typing the newsgroup name in the Discussion Group text box.

If no newsgroups are listed in the All Groups list box, this is the first time your computer has been used to access newsgroups. Click ⌈ Get Groups ⌋ to download the newsgroups from the news server. It will take a few minutes to get the entire newsgroup list.

The tabs in this dialog box can be used to list all available newsgroups, narrow newsgroups to descriptions that contain a keyword you specify, and list newsgroups created since you last listed available groups. The All Groups tab is open by default and displays the names of all newsgroups on the news server in the list box. To help locate newsgroups, Usenet has organized them into categories.

Concept 2: Categories of Newsgroups

Usenet organizes newsgroups into categories called **hierarchies**. There are about 30 major top-level hierarchies. The top-level hierarchy is then further subdivided into additional categories. The top seven hierarchies are often referred to as the "Big Seven." They are described below.

Hierarchy	Description
comp	Computers
misc	Discussions that do not fit anywhere else
news	Discussions about Usenet itself
rec	Recreation
soc	Social issues
sci	Science
talk	Controversial topics

In addition, one of the most popular top-level hierarchies beyond the Big Seven is alt (for alternative), which includes miscellaneous discussions that generally inspire a lot of different opinions.

Each newsgroup has a multi-part name that reflects the hierarchal organization. The names (from left to right as you read them) display the top-level hierarchy first, separated from the next (subtopic) by a dot, and so forth. Therefore, as you read the newsgroup name, the various parts of the name progressively narrow the topic of discussion. A sample of some newsgroups and what they discuss is shown below.

Newsgroup Name	Topic
alt.romance	Romance-related discussions, such as how to ask someone out
alt.tv.3rd-rock	*Third Rock from the Sun* television program
rec.food.recipes	Recipe exchange
rec.travel	Basic travel advice and tips
comp.unix.questions	Questions on the UNIX operating system
comp.windows	Discussions on the Windows operating system
comp.edu	Computer science education
soc.politics	Political problems, systems, solutions
soc.feminism	Feminism and feminist issues
news.announce.important	Important messages to all Usenet users
news.answers	FAQs (frequently asked questions) on Usenet
news.announce.newusers	Standard set of articles with general information about Usenet

Because the news administrator decides what newsgroups to carry, not all of these newsgroups listed may appear on your news server.

> The hierarchy list operates just like Window's Explorer window. Click the ⊞ to expand the groups and the ⊟ to collapse them.

You want to locate a newsgroup that discusses fitness topics. A good category to look for this group is the misc category. To see the newsgroups in this category,

■ Click the ⊞ next to the misc category.

Your screen should be similar to Figure 4-3.

FIGURE 4-3

indicates folder is expanded (open)   number of newsgroups in category   unsubscribed group   number of messages in group

> Scroll the list box to find this category. They are in alphabetical order. If your news server does not have this group, select a top-level category of your choice.

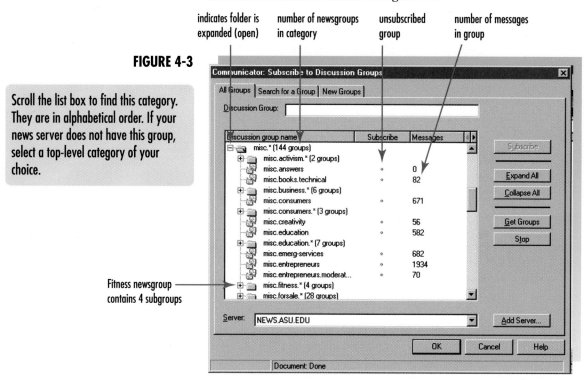

Fitness newsgroup contains 4 subgroups

The number in parenthesis indicates the number of newsgroups in the category. This misc. category includes more than 100 newsgroups, which are further divided into subgroups. The Subscribe column displays a checkmark if you are already subscribed to a group; otherwise it displays a dot. The Messages column shows the number of messages in the group. To subscribe to a fitness newsgroup,

■ Expand the misc.fitness group.

■ Select misc.fitness.aerobic.

■ Click Subscribe .

■ Click OK .

> A checkmark identifies the newsgroup to which you have subscribed.

Reading Newsgroup Messages

You are returned to the Netscape Message Center. Subscribing to a newsgroup adds the newsgroup to your personal list of newsgroups. The main reason for subscribing to newsgroups is to read the messages from other group members.

To see your list of subscribed newsgroups and to open the newsgroup to read the messages,

■ Expand your news server folder.

Your screen should be similar to Figure 4-4.

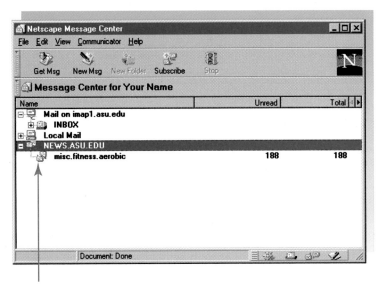

newsgroup that has been subscribed to

You can click the ⊞ or double-click the folder to expand it.

FIGURE 4-4

Your subscription list may include newsgroups that have already been subscribed to.

■ Double-click misc.fitness.aerobic.

If the newsgroup has more than 100 messages, a dialog box asks if you want to download all messages or just the first 50 or 100. If there are a lot of messages, it will take a long time to download them.

■ If necessary, select the option to limit the number of headers to download.

■ Click Download.

Your screen should be similar to Figure 4-5.

FIGURE 4-5

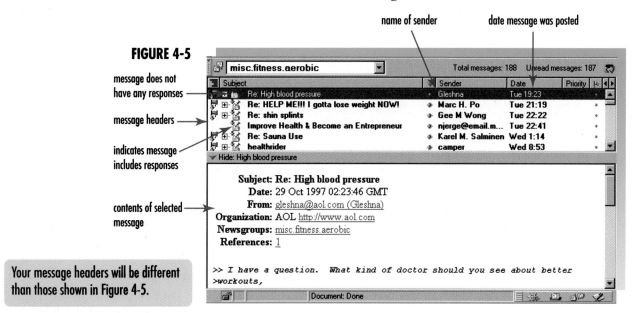

message does not have any responses

message headers

indicates message includes responses

contents of selected message

name of sender

date message was posted

Your message headers will be different than those shown in Figure 4-5.

You can size the panes by dragging the bar or hide the lower pane by clicking the ⬇.

The Discussion window is similar to the e-mail window. The message headers are displayed in the upper pane, and the current message is displayed in the lower pane. The header includes the topic for each message in the Subject column, the name of the person who submitted the message in the Sender column, and the date the message was posted in the Date column.

■   Scroll the upper pane to view additional message headers.

Message headers preceded with a 🖹 indicate that there are no responses to the message. Message headers preceded with a 🖭 indicate that there are responses to the original message. This creates a thread of topics in the newsgroup.

Concept 3: Thread

A **thread** is a newsgroup discussion about a specific topic with a common theme. Threads help organize subtopics in a newsgroup and are used to keep all the messages on the same subject together. When an original message is posted, it begins a new thread. All responses or follow-up messages are attached to the original so that you can read all the messages on the same subject one after the other.

■   Click on the ⊞ preceding any message to display the message thread.

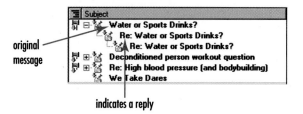

original message

indicates a reply

You will probably see several message subject headers that begin with "Re:". This indicates that the message is a response to an original message, thereby creating a discussion thread.

■   Click on an original message to read it and follow the thread through the replies.

Your screen should be similar to Figure 4-6.

The menu equivalent is **G**o/Next **U**nread Message, and the keyboard shortcut is **N**.

Clicking ⌨ displays the next unread message.

FIGURE 4-6

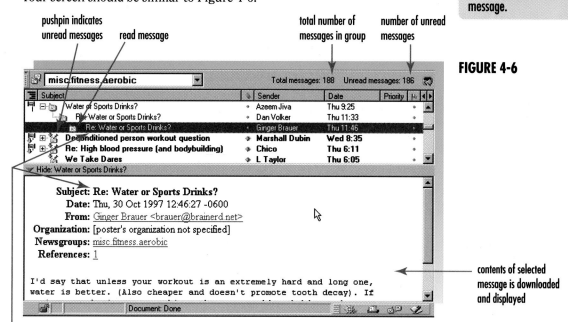

pushpin indicates unread messages   read message

total number of messages in group

number of unread messages

indicates a reply

contents of selected message is downloaded and displayed

As you select each message, the message's content is downloaded from the server and displayed in the lower pane. Also notice after you have selected a message, the red pushpin preceding the message header is no longer displayed. This indicates the message has been read. Additionally, the count of total and unread messages at the top of the window is updated. You can also manually mark a message as read or unread, mark a thread as read, mark all messages as read, and mark messages from a specific date as read or unread using the ⌨ button.

Posting a Message to a Newsgroup

As you read messages in a newsgroup, you may come across a question for which you have an answer or a topic on which you have an opinion. You may also have a new topic you want to discuss. Before posting to a newsgroup, you should be aware of the culture of the group.

Concept 4: Newsgroup Culture

Newsgroups tend to develop personalities over time. The members get to know one another and think of their group as a place where they can talk with friends. And much like any friendships, there are cliques with traditions. Before jumping in with questions or answers, it is a good idea to get a feel for the newsgroup first by reading messages for a few days. This is called **lurking**.

In addition, you may want to check out the newsgroup's **FAQ** (Frequently Asked Questions) article. This article contains answers to the group's most frequently asked questions. Reading the FAQ before posting a question saves the group from having to answer the same question repeatedly. FAQs also often include an explanation of abbreviations that you will frequently see used in the group. Some of the commonly used abbreviations and their meanings are listed below.

Abbreviation	Meaning
SO	Significant other
AFAIK	As far as I know
IMHO	In my humble opinion
OIC	Oh, I see!

Like e-mail, you will also find newsgroup messages that contain inflammatory remarks, called **flames**. This often leads to a thread called a **flame war**. When presented with a post that is meant to enrage you, the best thing is to ignore it and delete it. Another negative dynamic you will find in newsgroups is called **trolling**. This is the deliberate posting of a message containing incorrect information with the intent of receiving know-it-all replies.

Some other newsgroup terms are described in the table below.

Term	Meaning
Spamming	The annoying practice of sending junk e-mail (such as an advertisement) to newsgroups or mailing lists or to anyone you do not know.
RFD	Before a new group is created, Request for Discussion topics are proposed and voted on and will be widely propagated.
Saint	Someone who provides helpful information to new users and informs others of proper procedures within a group.
Wizard	Someone who has a great deal of knowledge about how things work.

Before posting a message to any newsgroup, you may want to practice the procedure first. For this purpose, many news servers offer a test newsgroup. To subscribe to a test newsgroup,

- Click [Netscape Message Ce...] in the taskbar to switch to the Message Center window.

- Click on your news server folder.

- Click [Subscribe].

- Subscribe to the misc.test newsgroup.

- Open the misc. test message newsgroup and download the first 50 or 100 message headers only.

To post a new message to this newsgroup,

- Click [New Msg].
- Maximize the window.

Your screen should be similar to Figure 4-7.

newsgroup address

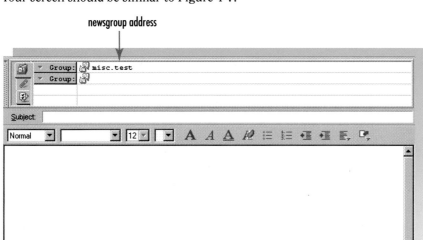

FIGURE 4-7

The Composition window is open. Creating a posting is similar to creating an e-mail message. It consists of header, subject, and message areas. And as with e-mail, there are some rules of etiquette that you should follow when posting a message.

> Your instructor will give you the name of the group if it is different from the one used in this text.

> You can also click 🔁 to switch to the Message Center window.

> The menu equivalent is **M**essage/**N**ew Message, and the keyboard shortcut is [Ctrl] + M.

Newsgroup Etiquette

In general, the same rules of etiquette apply to newsgroups as to e-mail. However, because you are posting to a public group, several other considerations should be kept in mind.

■ When posting replies, keep them brief and to the point, being particularly careful to stick to the topic thread.

■ Before you reply to a message, read the rest of the messages in the newsgroup to confirm that no one has already said what you want to say. If someone has, don't repeat it.

■ One of the biggest problems on Usenet is that a single question often receives many identical answers, unnecessarily overburdening the system. Instead, e-mail your answer directly to the person who asked the question and suggest that they summarize their responses to the group.

■ Likewise, when you post a question, suggest that answers be sent to your e-mail address and offer to summarize the answers to the group so others can benefit as well. The best way to summarize is to strip headers, combine duplicate information, and write a short summary. Try to credit the information to the people that sent it to you, where possible.

■ When replying to an article, summarize the parts of the article to which you are responding by including appropriate quotes from the original article. Then readers do not have to try to remember what the original article said.

Notice that the name of the newsgroup has already been entered for you in the header, just as when replying to an e-mail message. You can post a message to multiple groups by adding additional newsgroup addresses. This is just like sending the same e-mail message to multiple people.

The subject line is important to complete, because this line's content is what is displayed in the subject area of the message header. Because the subject line of a message is there to help a person decide whether or not to read your message, it is important that it be descriptive of the content of the message. In addition, it should be brief and to the point.

■ In the subject line type **Test Message Ignore**

By entering "ignore" in the subject line, you will not get an automatic e-mail reply from the newsgroup's news server. If you leave it out you may receive an e-mail message telling you that your test message was received.

The text of your posting is entered in the message area, just as if you were typing an e-mail message. Because most test messages are not read by anyone other than the original sender, if you ask a question you more than likely will not get an answer.

■ In the message area type **This is my test message**.

■ Click 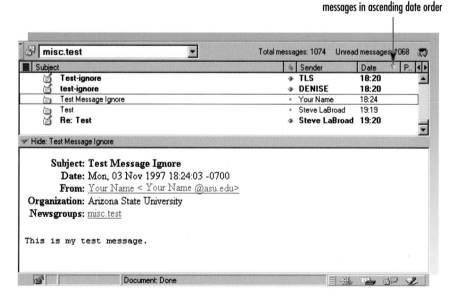 .

The message is sent to the news server and posted to the newsgroup to which it is directed. It may take seconds to hours or days before the message is displayed in the newsgroup. You can read your message in this newsgroup in the same way you read the messages in the first newsgroup you looked at. Just like other newsgroups, test messages are removed from the server periodically and can only be deleted by the server administrator or the person that posted the message. Because Usenet posts are intended for a public audience, never post anything you would not feel comfortable reading in the newspaper.

To remove a message, use **E**dit/Cancel Mess**a**ge or the keyboard shortcut ⌞Delete⌟.

To see the message you posted to the newsgroup,

■ Click .

The menu equivalent is **F**ile/Ge**t** Messages/**N**ew and the keyboard shortcut is ⌞Ctrl⌟ + T.

Any new messages sent to the newsgroup since you last opened it are added to the message header list. Since there are usually a large number of messages in a newsgroup, it could take a long time to locate one message or find the ones that relate to topics that interest you. Because of this you can sort the messages by subject, sender, date, or priority. Since you just recently sent your message, sorting by ascending date order should put your message at the bottom of the list. To sort the list by date,

The menu equivalent is **V**iew/S**o**rt/by Dat**e**/Ascending.

■ Click ⌞Date⌟ .

■ If necessary, select your message header to display your message.

The triangle symbol in the Date header will be ▾.

Your screen should be similar to Figure 4-8.

messages in ascending date order

FIGURE 4-8

Replying to a Newsgroup Message

As with e-mail, you can also reply to a newsgroup message. You can reply directly to the sender's e-mail address, to the sender and all other recipients' e-mail addresses, to the newsgroup, or to the sender and newsgroup. To reply only to the newsgroup,

■ Click .

■ Select Reply to Group.

■ Maximize the window.

> The menu equivalent is **M**essage/**R**eply/to **G**roup and the keyboard shortcut is Ctrl + D.

Reply to Sender	Ctrl+R
Reply to Sender and All Recipients	Ctrl+Shift+R
Reply to Group	
Reply to Sender and Group	

Notice that the address and subject lines have been completed for you, and the insertion point is waiting for you to enter additional information. The original message text appears preceded with a blue line. This distinguishes the original text from the new text you will enter. Your reply should be entered above the old text. To post and read your reply,

■ Type **Testing my reply**.

■ Press ←Enter twice.

■ Click Send .

> You may need to re-sort the newsgroup to locate your message.

■ Click Get Msg .

Your reply should be displayed in the newsgroup. Depending on the configuration of the newsgroup, your message may not appear as a thread. This happens in test areas because a lot of the messages have the same subject.

Unsubscribing to a Newsgroup

Since you no longer need the newsgroups, you will unsubscribe to them.

■ Switch to the Message Center window.

■ Right-click on the misc.test newsgroup name.

> The menu equivalent is **E**dit/**D**elete Discussion Group.

■ Choose **R**emove Discussion Group.

> If necessary, click OK in the warning dialog box.

■ Click OK .

■ Unsubscribe to the misc.fitness.aerobic newsgroup.

| Open Discussion Group |
| Open Discussion Group in New Window |
| New Message |
| Mark Discussion Group Read |
| Remove Discussion Group |
| Search Messages |
| Discussion Group Properties |

You can always resubscribe to a newsgroup again at any time if you later decide you want to check what is going on in the group.

After watching the information flow in various newsgroups for a while, you will feel comfortable posting your messages and questions. This may lead to gathering names and exchanging information with many people in different areas of the world. You can also print, copy, cut, and paste messages using the menu commands just as in other Windows applications.

Using News Search Sites

As you have seen, Usenet is a huge conglomeration of newsgroups with far ranging topics of discussion. Knowing which category to look in to locate a newsgroup you may be interested in is sometimes difficult. In addition, because postings are cleared periodically from the news server, you may miss a topic that was discussed that is of interest to you. To help find newsgroups and articles on specific topics, you can use a Web search site such as Deja News or AltaVista. To find other newsgroups that may be discussing aerobics, you will use AltaVista.

> You can also access a newsgroup by typing its URL in the location field. URLs for newsgroups begin with "news:" rather than "http:", followed by the newsgroup name. There is no server name or path.

- Click the Navigator button in the taskbar to switch back to the Navigator window.

- Click [Search].

- Click AltaVista.

- Select Usenet from the Search drop-down list box.

- Type **aerobics** in the search text box.

- Click [search].

- Scroll the window to see the search results.

> You may need to scroll to see the link.

Search the Web fo
 ├─ the Web ──── search drop-down list
 └─ Usenet
     ──── search text box

Your screen should be similar to Figure 4-9.

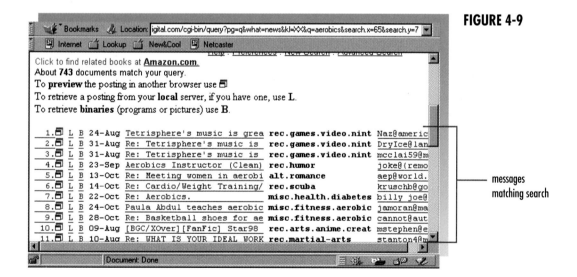

FIGURE 4-9

A list of messages matching your search query is displayed. The most relevant messages are at the top of the list. As you can see, the topic of aerobics was discussed in many other newsgroups in addition to the misc.fitness.aerobic newsgroup. To read a message, click on the subject link.

- Click on the subject of any article to read it.

- Click [Back] to return to the AltaVista search results page.

> You can click the newsgroup name to subscribe and view current articles.

In addition to reading postings, you can also reply directly to the sender by e-mail by clicking on their e-mail address link. This opens Netscape's composition window where you can create and send your message. You cannot, however, at this time reply to the newsgroup through AltaVista.

Finding Mailing Lists

Next you want to check out another popular type of discussion group, mailing lists, for discussions on fitness-related topics.

Concept 5: Mailing List

Mailing lists, also referred to simply as lists, consist of the e-mail addresses of a group of people who have subscribed to the mailing list because they are interested in the topic of the group. The messages are sent to a single e-mail address where they are then forwarded to each subscriber's e-mail inbox to read. There are roughly 40,000 mailing lists on specialized topics from environment to presidential politics to cooking. Each list has a set of subscribers, with varying levels of expertise and interest in the list topic. As with newsgroups, there are both moderated and unmoderated mailing lists.

Although most mailing lists are on the Internet, many are on the Bitnet, an academic network founded in 1981 to link universities by e-mail. The Internet and Bitnet networks are connected by a specialized computer called a **gateway**, which translates e-mail messages sent from one network into the protocol used on the other network. Because Bitnet relies heavily on e-mail to move information, you must communicate via e-mail to the mailing lists.

Most mailing lists are managed by automated computer programs, the most common of which is a **listserver**, called **listserv** for short. The listserv is responsible for the mechanics of accepting subscriptions to the list and of forwarding messages to subscribers on the list. It also allows subscribers to temporarily put a hold on deliveries and to unsubscribe from the list.

> Other mailing list computer programs are majordomo and listproc.

To subscribe to a list, you must locate the name of the list and the subscription address. One source of mailing list topics is through commercial publications, such as the Internet Yellow Pages published by McGraw-Hill. Several online sources are also available that provide mailing list topics. One such source is available by sending an e-mail message to listserv@listserv.net, a master list of mailing lists organized by topic. Leave the subject line of the message blank. At the top of the message body, enter "list global <topic>" where topic is a word or words describing the subject. For example, to get a list of mailing lists on space, you would enter "list global space." You will receive by e-mail a list of all known listservs relating to space.

You can also use the Web search engines to conduct a search for mailing lists on specific topics. There are also many Web pages devoted to maintaining a list of mailing lists on specific topics. See the following box of online mailing list sources.

Online Mailing List Sources

The following Web sites help you locate e-mail lists. Some offer keyword searching. Some provide information about the list, and some let you subscribe right from their Web site.

Web Site	Description
L-Soft Listserv Lists lsoft.com/lists/listref.html	Enables you to search for discussion lists by topic, name, or host sites. Includes a listing of lists with over 1,000 subscribers (not complete).
Interest Groups Finder alabanza.com/kabacoff/Inter-Links/listserv.html	Provides links to resources for finding e-mail discussion groups.
Tile.Net tile.net/tile/listserv/index.html	Browse lists alphabetically, by host country, see which ones are most popular, and conduct subject searches.
Liszt liszt.com/	A searchable directory of mailing lists with over 23,000 entries.
Searchable Mailing List Archives at Stanford University archive.stanford.edu/lists/	Excite-searchable indexes and hypermail archives.
Publicly Accessible Mailing Lists neosoft.com/cgi-bin/paml_search/	An up-to-date index of mailing lists arranged alphabetically by name and by subject.

You will use the L-Soft Listserv Lists Web site to locate a fitness-related mailing list. To access this page,

- Type **lsoft/lists/listref.html** in the Location text box.
- Press ←Enter.
- Click the Search for a mailing list of interest link.
- In the Look For text box, type **fitness**.
- Click [Start the search!].
- Click on the link to the search result, HEALTH-L@KSU.EDU.
- Scroll the page to see the information on how to subscribe.

If this URL does not work, try lsoft/catalist.html.

Your screen should be similar to Figure 4-10.

FIGURE 4-10

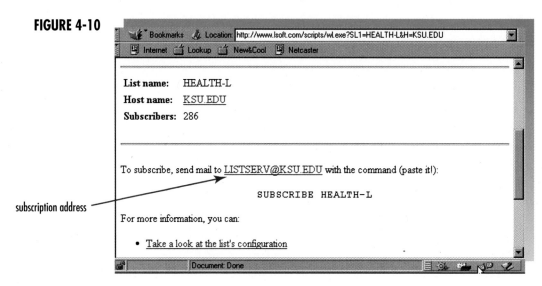

subscription address

This page includes information about the Kansas State University Health and Fitness mailing list, its size, and how to subscribe. This looks like a site that may be of interest to readers. Before recommending it, however, you want to subscribe to it so you can see what topics are being discussed.

Subscribing to a Mailing List

To participate in a mailing list, you first must become a member by subscribing to the list. You subscribe to a mailing list by sending an e-mail message to the subscription address.

Concept 6: Subscription Address and List Address

The **subscription address**, also commonly called a **listserv address**, of a mailing list is used to perform administrative tasks such as subscribing, unsubscribing, and requesting information from the listserv program. The subscription address consists of <listserv>@ followed by the listserv address. For example, listserv@ksu.edu is the subscription address for the Kansas State University Health and Fitness mailing list.

The **list address** of a mailing list is used to send a message to the members of the mailing list. The list address consists of <list name>@ followed by the last part of the subscription address. Health-L@ksu.edu is the list address for the Kansas State University Health and Fitness mailing list.

It is important to understand the difference between the listserv address and the mailing list address. You send commands to the listserv and posts to the mailing list address. Perhaps the most common problem on mailing lists is that people unintentionally send listserv commands to the mailing list address rather than to the listserv address. This fills up the mailing list with the electronic equivalent of junk mail that no one wants to see.

Those groups that are on the Bitnet use a Bitnet address. Bitnet addresses are different from Internet addresses in that they do not end in geographical or administrative domain names, such as .edu. Generally, all that is needed to send an e-mail message from the Internet to the Bitnet is to add .bitnet to the end of the address. Otherwise you may need to provide the name of the gateway computer and information about how to deliver the mail on Bitnet. Some Bitnet listservs are also connected to the Internet, so if you see a listserv address ending in .edu, you can e-mail the listserv without adding .bitnet to the end.

The Web page shows the subscription address for the fitness list is LISTSERV@KSU.EDU with the command SUBSCRIBE HEALTH-L. The command is entered in the body of your e-mail message and tells the listserver which mailing list you want to join. To subscribe, you can click the link in the Web page.

■   Click LISTSERV@KSU.EDU.

Your screen should be similar to Figure 4-11.

subscription address automatically inserted in Composition window

FIGURE 4-11

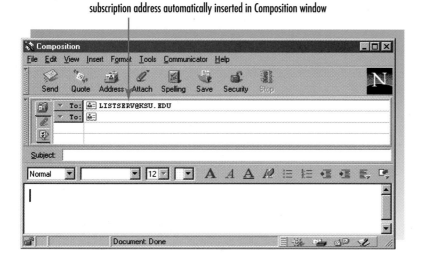

The Composition window is open, and the subscription address is automatically entered in the To line for you. In your e-mail subscription message, you enter the command to subscribe. When corresponding with the listserv, because you are communicating with a computer program, only certain commands are acknowledged. Because listserv programs vary, different commands may be used by different listservs. Many of the commands that can be used when sending an e-mail message to most listservs are listed below.

Listserv Command	Action
subscribe <listname>	Subscribes to list
unsubscribe <listname>	Unsubscribes to list
signoff<listname>	Unsubscribes to list
review <listname>	Requests a membership list
index <listname>	Requests names of files that are archived on the list
info <listname>	Requests information about the listserv
get <filename>	Requests a copy of an archived file
set <listname> nomail *or* postpone	Temporarily stops mail delivery
set <listname> mail *or* mailback	Begins mail delivery again after stopping
set <listname>repro	Has listserv send a copy of whatever you post to list

The most common command to begin a subscription is "subscribe." The command is followed by the name of the mailing list. The mailing list name for the fitness mailing list is Health-L. In some cases the mailing list name is then followed by your name. Do not use your e-mail address, because the listserv gets it from your message header. To enter the command and send the message,

■ Type **subscribe health-l** in the message text area.

> You can move the Composition window to see the instructions in the Navigator window on how to subscribe.

Your screen should be similar to Figure 4-12.

subject left blank

FIGURE 4-12

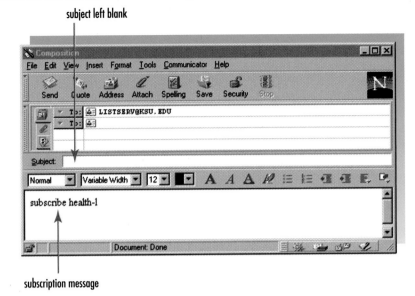

subscription message

The subscription message is complete.

■ Click ![Send] to send the message.

You are asked if you want to include a subject. When subscribing to mailing lists, the subject line is ignored, so leave it blank.

■ Click ![OK].

Generally, in a matter of a few minutes, you will receive any number of different e-mail responses back from the listserv. One message may tell what computer resources were used to process your subscription. There may be an interim message telling you that your subscription request has been received and that it will be processed shortly or that it is being forwarded. If your subscription request contained an error, you will receive a message indicating what is wrong. In that case, you would need to resubmit your request. Some mailing lists send a message asking you to send a confirmation response to the listserv. If you receive this type of message, you would need to follow the instructions to confirm your subscription.

■ While waiting for your reply, open your inbox and get your incoming mail messages.

Note: If you do not receive a reply in 10 minutes, continue reading the information in this section. Before ending the lab, check your inbox for replies to your subscription request and perform the instructions in this section.

The Mailbox button on the Component bar will alert you when a new message has been received by displaying a green dot. Netscape Messenger checks your server periodically for new mail (every 10 minutes is the default). To check for messages more frequently, click ![Get Msg].

If your subscription request to the fitness mailing list went through without any problems, you will receive a reply rather quickly. This message will be a confirmation message.

■ When you have received a new message(s), read the command confirmation request message.

Your screen should be similar to Figure 4-13.

FIGURE 4-13

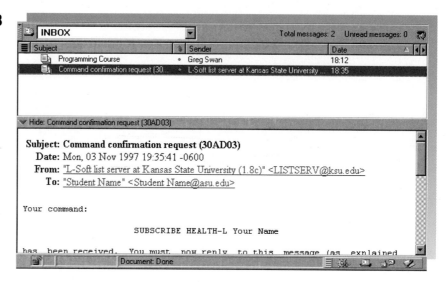

Because we do not want to clutter the mailing list with unnecessary subscriptions, you will not send in the confirmation. Your request will then be canceled automatically when no response is received within 24 hours.

If you had confirmed the request, you would receive two more replies. The first message would indicate that you have been added to the Health-L list. The second message would welcome you to the list and provide additional information about the list, including information on how to unsubscribe. You always want to save a copy of this message so you will know how to unsubscribe to the list at a later time.

■ Print a copy of your confirmation message, then delete it.

■ Close the Messenger window.

Once you have subscribed, your e-mail address is added to the list of subscribers to the mailing list and you will receive copies of all e-mail messages sent to the mailing list. Depending on how active the list is, you may begin receiving messages immediately and you may find that your inbox is flooded with e-mail messages from the mailing list. When you first subscribe, you may want to observe and find out what the list is about before participating. Each list has its own personality.

After waiting a few days and reading some of the messages you receive from the mailing list, if you find you are interested in a topic, post a message to the mailing list (use the list address). In this case, you would address your e-mail message to Health-L@KSU.edu. Remember, this address is different from the subscription address. Try not to confuse the two. Otherwise you may find that you have sent a message to subscribe to all members of the group. Any e-mail messages you send to the list will be sent to all list members unless you address the message to an individual. As with newsgroups, there are certain rules of etiquette that should be followed when posting a message to a mailing list.

Mailing List Etiquette

When corresponding in a mailing list, keep the following rules of etiquette in mind:

- Keep your questions and comments relevant to the focus of the list.

- Remember, what you say is seen by all members of the list. If your reply would have meaning only to the sender of an e-mail message, send your reply to the individual rather than to the list.

- Keep the number of lists you subscribe to small. The messages from various listservs require extensive system processing and can tie up computer resources. In addition, your mailbox may suddenly become very full.

- When asking a question, you can request that responses be sent to you personally rather than to the list. Then you can compile a summary of the answers to share with the entire list if you want.

- When replying, check that your response is going to the correct location, that is, to the list or the individual.

- When you go on vacation, unsubscribe or suspend mail delivery.

It is possible that a topic you are interested in may have already been discussed, and someone may refer you to a past posting on the list. Many of these past postings are saved (archived) by the listserv. Requesting an information sheet from the listserv will usually provide instructions on how to access archived postings (see command list on page 132).

If you are not interested in the mailing list, send a message back to the subscription address unsubscribing to the list.

Joining a Chat Discussion

Another way to communicate on the Internet is in chat groups.

Concept 7: Chat Group

Communicating in a **chat group** means carrying on a conversation live (in real time) with other people over the Internet. The most common chat system is **Internet relay chat (IRC)**, in which users communicate in discussion areas called **channels** or rooms. There is no restriction to the number of people that can participate in a given discussion, or the number of channels that can be formed over IRC. Before you can talk on IRC, you must have a chat client installed on your computer system. IRC clients have been developed for a variety of computer systems and are available for download from the Internet.

There are also several other types of Web-based, non-IRC chat systems. Although the commands and procedures may differ among them, the underlying principles are the same.

Chatting has been used extensively for live coverage of world events, news, sports commentary, and so on. It also serves as an inexpensive substitute for long-distance calling.

> Your instructor will inform you if you are to complete this section. If you cannot complete this section, read about chatting and try it when you have a computer of your own.

To demonstrate chatting, you will use the chat group provided by Yahoo.

- Click [Search].

- Click **Yahoo**.

- Click Chat.

Your screen should be similar to Figure 4-14.

FIGURE 4-14

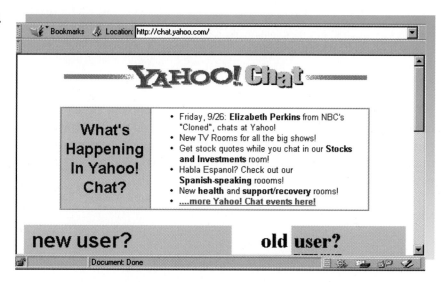

> You may be advised that you need to download the Yahoo chat client before you can register. Ask your instructor for permission to download the client before continuing.

First you need to register as a new chat user with Yahoo. This will require that you enter a user name and password.

- Click [GET REGISTERED] and follow the instructions to register.

- Click [I Accept] to accept the Yahoo! Chat agreement terms.

The Yahoo Chat screen should be similar to Figure 4-15.

areas of chat groups

FIGURE 4-15

Once you are registered, you can sign on and choose a chat channel. By entering your user name and password, you will be able to select from hundreds of chat channels on many different subjects.

■   Select an area of interest to you.

■   Click   Start Chatting .

The Yahoo Chat screen will look similar to Figure 4-16.

conversation scrolls
in chat room

people participating
in chat room

FIGURE 4-16

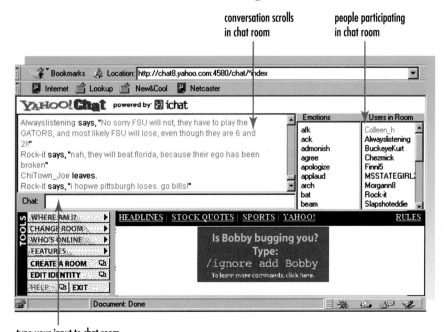

type your input to chat room

The top left half of the window displays the conversation, and the top right lists the names of the users on this chat channel. If this is your first time on a chat channel, you should read the messages being displayed and read the Help files for more information about chatting on the Internet. Once you feel comfortable with chatting, it can be a fun and rewarding experience.

- Clear ⌧EXIT⌧ to exit the chat group.

- Close all Netscape windows and, if necessary, disconnect from the Internet.

LAB REVIEW

Key Terms

article (NET114)	Internet relay chat (IRC) (NET136)	news server (NET114)
channel (NET136)	list address (NET131)	post (NET114)
chat group (NET136)	listserv address (NET131)	subscribe (NET115)
Collabra (NET114)	listserver (listserv) (NET128)	subscription address (NET131)
discussion group (NET113)	lurk (NET122)	thread (NET120)
FAQ (NET122)	mailing list (NET128)	troll (NET122)
flame (NET122)	moderated (NET114)	unmoderated (NET114)
flame war (NET122)	newsgroup (NET114)	Usenet (NET114)
gateway (NET128)	newsgroup site (NET114)	
hierarchy (NET117)	newsreader program (NET114)	

Command Summary

Command	Shortcut	Button	Action
Communicator/Collabra **D**iscussion Groups			Opens Collabra component
File/Ge**t** Messages/**N**ew	Ctrl + T	Get Msg	Displays all new message headers
File/Su**b**scribe to Discussion Groups		Subscribe	Subscribes to selected newsgroup
Edit/Cancel Mess**a**ge	Delete		Deletes posted message
Edit/**D**elete Discussion Group			Removes subscribed newsgroup
Go/Next **U**nread Message	N	Next	Displays next unread message
Message/**R**eply/to **G**roup	Ctrl + D	Reply	Creates a reply message to newsgroup

Matching

1. listserv address   _____   **a.** used to separate topics in a newsgroup name

2. unsubscribe   _____   **b.** rules used to communicate over Internet

3. list address   _____   **c.** indicates a follow-up article

4. subscribe   _____   **d.** common theme discussions

5. . (dot)   _____   **e.** address used to perform mailing list administrative tasks

6. protocol   _____   **f.** a collection of newsgroups

7. post   _____   **g.** to remove a newsgroup or mailing list

8. threads   _____   **h.** address used to send or post messages to mailing list

9. Usenet   _____   **i.** to add a newsgroup or mailing list

10. Re: _____   **j.** to send a message to a newsgroup or mailing list

Fill-In Questions

1. Using the screen below, enter the correct term for each item.

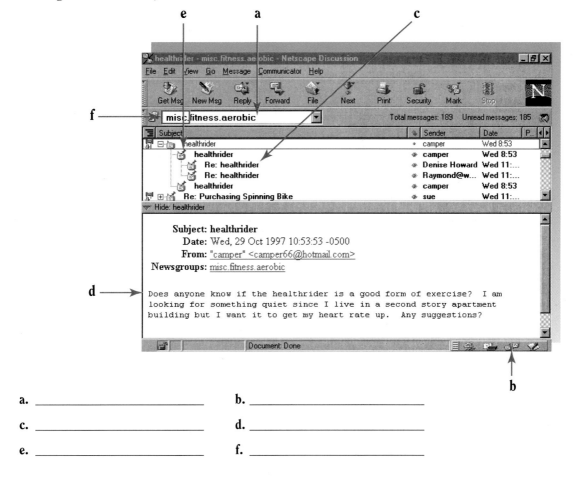

a. _____   b. _____

c. _____   d. _____

e. _____   f. _____

2. Using the screen below, enter the correct term for each item.

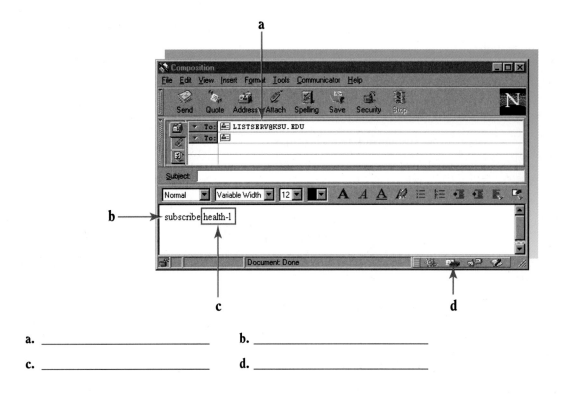

a. _____   b. _____

c. _____   d. _____

Short-Answer Questions

1. What is a newsgroup? What is a mailing list?
2. What does it mean to subscribe to a newsgroup?
3. What is the difference between a moderated and unmoderated group?
4. What do the parts of newsgroup names separated by dots signify?
5. What different ways can you respond to a newsgroup article?
6. How do you send a new article to a newsgroup?
7. How do you subscribe to a mailing list?
8. Discuss why it is important to follow etiquette when posting messages to newsgroups and mailing lists.

Hands-On Practice Exercises

On Your Own

Rating System	
	Easy
☆☆	Moderate
☆☆☆	Difficult

1. Find the names of two newsgroups on the topic of computers. Describe the types of articles sent to these groups.

2. Find a newsgroup about the state or country you live in. What is the name of this newsgroup? What types of topics are discussed in this group? Select a topic and describe the types of postings that it contains.

3. Using the list of mailing lists shown in the box on page 143, join a group. Check for messages frequently and remember to unsubscribe or suspend your mail when you are not able to check messages.

4. Locate a newsgroup on a topic that interests you. Read the messages and write a short summary of what types of messages are posted. Discuss how questions and comments are answered and if this group seems to follow the rules of etiquette discussed in the lab.

5. Microsoft has their own chat system, formerly called Comic Chat and now simply Microsoft Chat. Learn about this chat system at http://www.microsoft.com/ie/chat. What is different about this chat system? Describe several of its features.

6. Subscribe to a newsgroup of your choice, read and post messages to it.

7. Try the chat rooms at http://www.acmepet.com for live conversations all about different types of pets.

8. Hot Wired, a popular Web site, has a chat system at http://www.talk.com. Use the Enter link to get on, register, and then follow the procedures to participate in a chat group.

9. Using one of the online mailing list sources (page 129), locate a mailing list on a topic of interest. Subscribe to the list. Check for messages frequently and remember to unsubscribe or suspend your mail when you are not able to check messages.

10. Locate a mailing list and newsgroup that discuss the same issues. Write a summary report on what types of messages are sent to the mailing list and newsgroup. Discuss how the messages are similar and how they are different. Recommend the appropriate list for people with varying interests.

A Newsgroup Sampling

Category	Newsgroup Name	Discussion Area
Business	misc.invest	Investments
	misc. entrepreneurs	Owning your own business
College	alt.college.us	Rumors and reputations of various schools
	soc.college	College activities
Comics	rec.arts.comics.xbooks	X-men comics
	alt.comics.batman	Batman comics
	alt.comics.superman	Superman comics
Dance	rec.art.dance	General dance
Drama	rec.art.theater.plays	Theater and drama
Food and drink	rec.crafts.brewing	Beer brewing
	rec.food.historic	History of food
	alt.food.ice-cream	Ice cream
Fun	alt.religion.santaism	Santa Claus
	rec.rollercoaster	Fans of roller coasters exchange experiences
Games	alt.atari-jaguar.discussion	Video games
	rec.games.video.nintendo	Nintendo video games
Government	clari.news.usa.gov.white_house	White House news
Health	alt.support.diet	Dieting support
	clari.tw.health	Health care and medicine
Hobbies	rec.radio.amateur.equipment	Equipment for amateur radios
	rec.antiques	Buy, sell, and trade antiques
	rec.juggling	Juggling oranges, numbers, etc.
	rec.crafts.quilting	Quilting
Home	alt.home.repair	Home repair
	alt.hoovers	Vacuum cleaners
Humor	alt.humor.puns	Word play
Jobs	bionet.jobs.wanted	Biological sciences jobs
	misc.jobs.offered.entry	Entry-level jobs
	misc.jobs.resumes	Posted resumes
Medicine	alt.med.allergy	Causes and treatments for allergies
	sci.med.dentistry	Dentistry
Music	rec.music.classical	Classical music
	rec.music.marketplace	Buy or sell musical instruments, equipment, records, etc.
	rec.music.compose	Compose original music
Pets	alt.aquaria	Tropical fish
	rec.equestrian	Horse lovers

A Newsgroup Sampling (continued)

Category	Newsgroup Name	Discussion Area
	rec.pets.birds	Advice and anecdotes on birds
	rec.pets.cats	Advice and anecdotes on cats
	rec.pets.dogs	Advice and anecdotes on dogs
Science	sci.astro.planetarium	Planetarium programs
	bionet.cellbiol	Cell biology
	alt.energy.renewable	Renewable energy
Travel	rec.travel.france	Travel information on France
	rec.travel.air	Deals on air tickets and other bargains
	rec.travel.marketplace	Deals on air tickets and other bargains

A Mailing List Sampling

Topic	Subscription Address (listserv@)	List Name
ER-television	gcp.thenorth.com	er-l
Jag-television	american.edu	jagtv-l
College Bowl discussion	listserv.rice.edu	cb-l
Ceramic arts	lsv.uky.edu	clayart
Theatre and musical artists	lists.psu.edu	collab-l
D+D cartoons	netspace.org	d+d-cartoon
Earthsave discussion	maelstrom.stjohns.edu	earthsave
Shark and cartilaginous fish	raven.utc.edu	shark-l
Rare books	listserv.indiana.edu	rarebook-l
Discussion of books by Anne Rice	lists.psu.edu	arbooks
Sociology and computers discussion	vm.temple.edu	asascan
Use of computers in sport	listserv.unb.ca	sportpc
Advanced manufacturing methods	vm.its.rpi.edu	amm-l
Computer-aided design and manufacturing	listserv.syr.edu	cadam-l
Movie poster discussion	american.edu	mopo-l
Internet in business discussion list	listserv.aol.com	inbusiness
Internet and Computer Law Association	lists.ufl.edu	intlaw-l
Food and wine discussion	cmuvm.csv.cmich.edu	foodwine
Exercise and sports psychology	vm.temple.edu	sportpsy
Women in Sports and Physical Activity Journal list	listserv.uta.edu	wspaj-l
Exercise/diet/wellness list	etsuadmn.bitnet	fit-l

████ ████ ████ ████ ████ ████ ████ ░░░ ░░░ ░░░

Communicating with Newsgroups, Mailing Lists, and Chats

Categories of Newsgroups

Usenet organizes newsgroups into categories called hierarchies.

Newsgroup

Newsgroups are special interest groups that are part of the network news system called Usenet, a network dedicated exclusively to the dissemination of newsgroup messages.

Thread

A thread is a newsgroup discussion about a specific topic with a common theme.

Newsgroup Culture

Newsgroups tend to develop personalities over time. The members get to know one another and think of their group as not just a location, but a place where they can talk with friends.

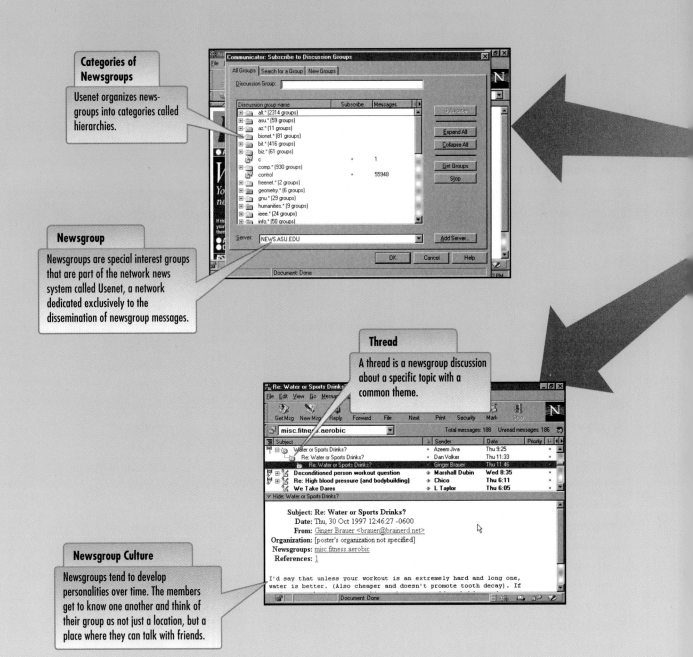

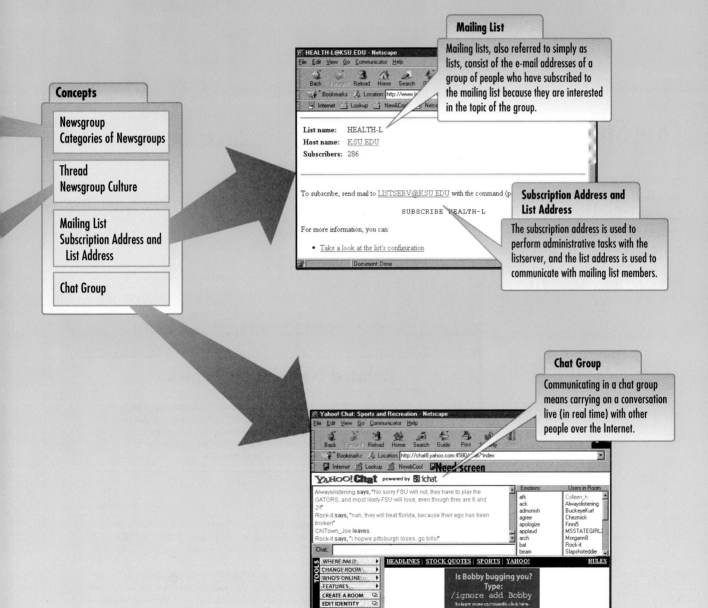

Concepts

Newsgroup
Categories of Newsgroups

Thread
Newsgroup Culture

Mailing List
Subscription Address and
    List Address

Chat Group

Mailing List

Mailing lists, also referred to simply as lists, consist of the e-mail addresses of a group of people who have subscribed to the mailing list because they are interested in the topic of the group.

HEALTH-L@KSU.EDU - Netscape

File Edit View Go Communicator Help

Back Forward Reload Home Search

Bookmarks Location: http://www.k

Internet Lookup New&Cool Netsc

List name: HEALTH-L

Host name: KSU.EDU

Subscribers: 286

To subscribe, send mail to LISTSERV@KSU.EDU with the command (p

SUBSCRIBE HEALTH-L

For more information, you can:

• Take a look at the list's configuration

Document: Done

Subscription Address and List Address

The subscription address is used to perform administrative tasks with the listserver, and the list address is used to communicate with mailing list members.

Chat Group

Communicating in a chat group means carrying on a conversation live (in real time) with other people over the Internet.

Yahoo! Chat: Sports and Recreation - Netscape

File Edit View Go Communicator Help

Back Forward Reload Home Search Guide Print Stop

Bookmarks Location: http://chat8.yahoo.com:4580/*al/*index

Internet Lookup New&Cool **Need** screen

YAHOO! Chat powered by ichat

Alwayslistening says, "No sorry FSU will not, they have to play the GATORS, and most likely FSU will lose, even though they are 6 and 2!!"
Rock-it says, "nah, they will beat florida, because their ego has been broken"
ChiTown_Joe leaves.
Rock-it says, "i hopwe pittsburgh loses. go bills!"

Chat:

Emotions	Users in Room
afk	Colleen_h
ack	Alwayslistening
admonish	BuckeyeKurt
agree	Chezmick
apologize	Finni5
applaud	MSSTATEGIRL2
arch	Morgann8
bat	Rock-it
beam	Slapshoteddie

TOOLS
WHERE AM I?
CHANGE ROOM
WHO'S ONLINE
FEATURES
CREATE A ROOM
EDIT IDENTITY
HELP EXIT

HEADLINES | STOCK QUOTES | SPORTS | YAHOO!   RULES

Is Bobby bugging you?
Type:
/ignore add Bobby
To learn more commands, click here.

Document: Done

Creating Web Pages

COMPETENCIES

After completing this lab, you will know how to:

1. Design a Web page.
2. Enter page content.
3. Format text.
4. Apply character effects.
5. Add a background.
6. Insert an image.
7. Preview a Web page.
8. Add rules.
9. Create a bulleted list.
10. Create links.
11. Publish a Web page.

Case Study

You have met with the Web site administrator and discussed the steps you need to take to create the new Web page of related links to the newsletter articles. Your next step is to convert the text document of links to a Web page. Web pages can take minutes to hours to create depending upon the complexity of the page design. This lab will discuss some of the fundamentals of designing and creating a Web page using Netscape Communicator's Composer component.

You have been asked to develop an overall design and layout for the new Web page. Your completed Web page will look like that shown below.

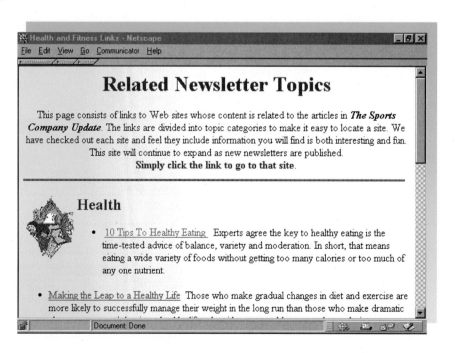

Concept Overview

The following concepts will be introduced in this lab:

1. Web Page Design
There are many elements that can be added to a Web page to make it attractive and easy to use. Graphic objects, images, art, and color are perhaps the most important features of Web pages.

2. HTML Tags
HTML tags are embedded codes that supply information about the page's structure, appearance, and contents.

3. Fonts
A font, also commonly referred to as a typeface, is a set of characters with a specific design.

4. Paragraph Alignment
Alignment is how text is positioned on a line between the margins or indents. There are three types of paragraph alignment: left, center, and right.

5. Character Effects
Different character effects such as bold, italics, and color can be applied to selections to add emphasis or interest to a page.

6. Images
Authors use images in Web pages to provide information or decoration, or to communicate their personal or organizational style.

7. Absolute and Relative Links
When you create a hyperlink in a Web page, you can make the path to the destination of the hyperlink an absolute link or a relative link.

Designing a Web Page

You have discussed the purpose of the new Web page with Donna Blackcloud, the site administrator. She suggested that you create the new Web page of related links using the **Composer** component that is included with the Netscape Communicator program.

- Start Netscape Communicator.

- Click ✎ Composer in the Component Bar.

- If necessary, maximize the Composer window.

> If you are working on a computer with a modem, you can choose **F**ile/Go **O**ffline from the Navigator window to disconnect from the Internet. The lab will instruct you when you need to go back online.

Your screen should be similar to Figure 5-1.

FIGURE 5-1

Composition toolbar →

Formatting toolbar →

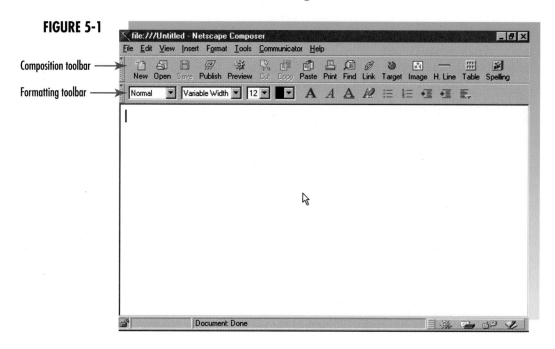

The Composer window includes menus, commands, and options that provide the tools you will need to create a Web page. In addition, it includes a Composition toolbar and a Formatting toolbar that contain shortcuts for many of the menu options.

> The Formatting toolbar contains the same buttons as in the Messenger composition window.

When creating or **authoring** a Web page, you want to make the page both attractive and informative. You also want it to be easy to use and you want it to work right. It is important, therefore, to plan the design of the Web site and the pages it will include in advance.

Concept 1: Web Page Design

There are many elements that can be added to a Web page to make it attractive and easy to use. Graphic objects, images, art, and color are perhaps the most important features of Web pages. They entice the user to continue to explore the Web site. Other elements, such as animations, scrolling banners, blinking text, audio, and video can be added to a Web page to make it even more dynamic.

With all these elements, it is easy to add too many to a page and end up with a cluttered and distracting mess. Keep the following design tips in mind when authoring your own Web pages.

- The text content of your page is the single most important element. Text should be readable against the background. Check for proper spelling and grammar.

- Background colors and patterns add interest and pizzazz to a page, but be careful that they do not make the page hard to read. Additionally, keep in mind that more complex patterns take longer to download. Also, since many users have 256-color monitors, higher resolution colors will be lost and may not look good on their monitors.

- Keep graphics and animations simple to speed up downloading, and avoid busy animations and blinking text. A good suggestion is to keep images less than 100k in file size. Smaller is even better.

- Page dimensions should be the same as the browser window size. Because many users have their screen resolution set to 640 by 480 pixels, designing a page for 600 by 800 pixels will be too large for their screens.

- In general, keep your page length no longer than two to three 640 by 480 screens' worth of information. If a page is too long, the reader has to remember too much information that has scrolled off the screen.

- At the bottom of each page, include navigation links back to the home page and other major site pages so users will not get lost. Also include text links for users who have turned off graphics loading in their browsers to improve downloading speed.

- Because not all browsers support all HTML features, do not make your document overly dependent on HTML features that cannot be seen by all browsers. For example, some browsers might not accept your graphics or animations, in which case you would want to provide alternative text.

- Although frames can make navigation in your Web site easier, too many can make it difficult to read the screen. Use the minimum number of frames possible. Many browsers cannot display frames, so you may want to consider creating a non-frame version to accommodate those users.

- Get permission before using text, sounds, and images that are copyrighted. Copyright laws and infringement fines apply to pages posted on the Internet.

The site administrator suggested using the same basic layout and colors that are used in other pages in the site to maintain a unified look. In addition, since the site will be mostly text links, she suggested that you include a graphic image or animation to make the site more interesting to view. After considering these features, you drew a sample page layout that you feel may be both interesting and easy to use.

Entering the Page Content

As you learned in Lab 1, all pages on the WWW are written using a programming language called HTML (HyperText Markup Language). Every item on a Web page has properties associated with it that are encoded in HTML tags.

Concept 2: HTML Tags

HTML **tags** are embedded codes that supply information about the page's structure, appearance, and contents. They tell your browser where the title, heading, paragraphs, images, links, bold text, listings, and other information are to appear on the page. In addition, they designate links to other Web pages. Tags usually appear on either side of the selected text and consist of two parts. The first part tells where to begin the feature and second part tells where to end it. A slash (/) in the ending tag means "end command." All tags are surrounded by the less-than and greater-than symbols (<>). Only the selected text appears in the format specified by the tag. Tags do not show when you load the HTML page on your browser. Examples of some simple tags and their effects are shown below.

Tagged text	Effect
<B> Hello </B>	Bolds the word **Hello**
<P> text </P>	Marks the beginning and end of a paragraph
<TITLE>The Sports Company</TITLE>	Displays text as a title

All Web pages commonly include a title, different levels of headings, and text design elements such as horizontal rules. Each of these elements has its own tag.

Netscape's Composer is an authoring tool that lets you create a Web page without needing to know the HTML codes. It makes it easy to create and design a page by generating the HTML tags automatically while you are using many of the same features you would use in a word processor to create a text document.

Composer offers several ways to create Web pages. You can edit a Web page you are viewing in the Navigator window or a page you have saved as an HTML file on your disk using the Composer window. You can also use the Page Wizard to help you quickly create a Web page. The Page Wizard is an interactive page on the Netscape home site that provides step-by-step directions to help you create a Web page. You complete each step by entering text, selecting colors, and adding elements such as lines and bullets. When you have completed the steps, you have the basics for a page that you can further refine using the Composer window. Another way is to select a predesigned Web page template available from the Netscape Template Web site and edit it to suit your needs. Finally, you can start from scratch with a blank Web page. This is the method you will use.

First you will enter a page title and introductory paragraphs. Entering text in Composer is very much like entering text in most word processing applications. The insertion point is positioned at the top of the Composer window, ready for you to begin to type.

> The Netscape Template Web Site and Page Wizard are located on the Netscape home site. You must be online to use these features.

- Type **Related Newsletter Topics**

- Press ⎡←Enter⎤ twice.

- Type **This page consists of links to Web sites whose content is related to the articles in The Sports Company Update. The links are divided into topic categories to make it easy to locate a site. We have checked out each site and feel they include information you will find is both interesting and fun. This site will continue to expand as new newsletters are published.**

- Press ⎡⇧Shift⎤ + ⎡←Enter⎤.

- Type **Simply click the link to go to that site.**

- Press ⎡←Enter⎤ twice.

> Using ⎡⇧Shift⎤ + ⎡←Enter⎤ inserts a new line break to continue text on the next line without creating a new paragraph.

Your screen should be similar to Figure 5-2.

checks spelling of Web page

FIGURE 5-2

page title →

introductory paragraph

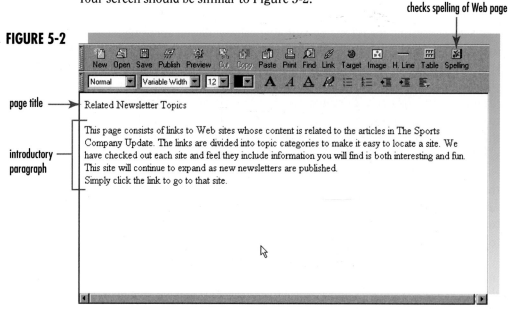

To check your typing, you will use the Spelling Checker. This is the same tool you used in the Messenger Composition window to check the spelling of your e-mail message.

■ Click [Spelling] to check the spelling of your page content and make corrections as needed.

So far this page looks like any other text document. However, as you entered the text, Composer included the necessary HTML tags. To see the HTML code,

■ Choose **V**iew/Page So**u**rce.

Your screen should be similar to Figure 5-3.

HTML tag identifies file type →

head tag identifies author

body tag identifies the content of the page

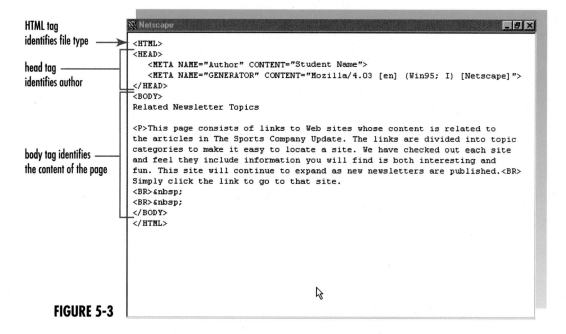

FIGURE 5-3

A second window is open that displays the contents of the page and its HTML coding. All HTML document files begin with the <HTML> tag that tells the browser that the document it is reading is an HTML document. They also contain a <HEAD> tag, which includes basic information needed by the browser, and a <BODY> tag, which indicates the area where the body of the page will appear. Each paragraph begins with a <P> tag.

■ Click ⊠ to close this window.

To complete entering the text for the page, you will copy the information from the Related Links file into the Composer document. This file is similar to the Newsletter Links file you created in Lab 2, but includes more descriptive summaries and a consistent layout.

■ Open the text file Related Links.rtf using WordPad or any word processor.

■ Select the entire document.

Use **E**dit/Select **A**ll or drag to select the document.

■ Click 🖺 Copy.

■ Click ⊠ to close the file and exit the program.

■ If necessary, move the insertion point to the last blank line below the text you entered in Composer.

■ Click 📋 Paste .

■ Move to the top of the document.

Your screen should be similar to Figure 5-4.

FIGURE 5-4

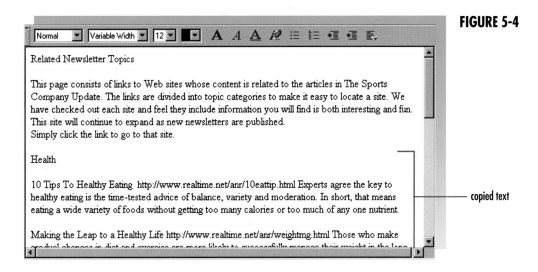

copied text

Now that the content of the page is complete, you are ready to enhance the appearance of the page.

Formatting Text

Composer includes two types of format styles, paragraph and character. Paragraph formats consist of combinations of formats that affect all paragraphs in the selection or the paragraph in which the insertion point is located. Character formats are formats such as font types, styles, sizes, and colors that affect the selected text only. When text is first entered in a blank HTML document, it is formatted using the default paragraph style of Normal. This sets the font type to Variable Width and the font size to 12 points.

> Composer's default font setting of Variable Width instructs the browser that is displaying the page to use its selected variable width font.

Concept 3: Fonts

A **font**, also commonly referred to as a **typeface**, is a set of characters with a specific design. The designs have names such as Times New Roman and Courier New. Using fonts as a design element can add interest to your page and give readers visual cues to help them find information quickly. It is good practice to use only two types of fonts in a document, one for text and one for headers. Too many font styles can make your document look cluttered and unprofessional.

Some fonts, such as Courier New, are **fixed**, which means that each character takes up the same amount of space. Most fonts are **variable**, which means that some letters, such as m or w, take up more space than other letters, such as i or t. Arial and Times New Roman are variable fonts.

Each font has one or more sizes. Size is the height and width of the character and is commonly measured in **points**, abbreviated "pt." One point equals about 1/72 of an inch, and text in most documents is 10 pt or 12 pt.

Several common fonts in different sizes are shown in the following table.

Font Name	Font Size
Arial	This is 10 pt. This is 16 pt.
Courier New	This is 10 pt. This is 16 pt.
Times New Roman	This is 10 pt. This is 16 pt.

HTML converts point sizes to the closest HTML size, a range from 1 to 7. The HTML range instructs the browser to display the text within the tag in the specified HTML size. The font may not appear in the specified size if the browser's font preferences are different.

First you will change the page title to the Heading paragraph style. Headings make it easier to locate information on a page by visually dividing it into sections. The six heading levels differ from normal text by their type size. The most important heading on your page should be assigned a Heading 1 level, the next most important a Heading 2 level, and so on.

- Click on the page title.

- Click [Normal ▼] to open the Paragraph style drop-down list.

- Click Heading 1.

> The menu equivalent is **F**ormat/**H**eading.

Normal ▼
Normal
Heading 1
Heading 2
Heading 3
Heading 4
Heading 5
Heading 6
Address
Formatted
List Item
Desc. Title
Desc. Text

Your screen should be similar to Figure 5-5.

FIGURE 5-5

text formatted
in Heading 1 style

Aligning Paragraphs

Next you want to change the alignment of the page title so it is centered on the page.

Concept 4: Paragraph Alignment

Alignment is how text is positioned on a line between the margins or indents. There are three types of paragraph alignment: left, center, and right.

Alignment		Effect on Text
Left		Aligns text against the left margin of the page, leaving the right margin ragged. This is the most commonly used paragraph alignment type and therefore the default setting.
Center		Centers each line of text between left and right margins. Center alignment is used mostly for headings or centering graphics on a page.
Right		Aligns text against right margin, leaving left margin ragged. Use right alignment when you want text to line up on the outside of a page, such as a chapter title or a header.

- If necessary, move the insertion point to the page title.

- Click [icon] Alignment.

- Click [icon] Center.

The title is now centered on the line between the left and right margins.

The menu equivalent is **F**ormat/**A**lign/**C**enter and the keyboard shortcut is [Ctrl] + **E**.

Applying Character Effects

You also want to add color to the page title. Color is one of several character formats that can be used to enhance the appearance of text in a Web page.

Concept 5: Character Effects

Different character effects such as bold, italics, and color can be applied to selections to add emphasis or interest to a page. The table below describes the effects and their uses.

Format	Example	Use
Bold	**Bold**	Adds emphasis
Italic	*Italic*	Adds emphasis
Underline	<u>Underline</u>	Adds emphasis
Superscript	"To be or not to be."[1]	Used in footnotes and formulas
Subscript	H_2O	Used in formulas
Non-breaking	Text does not wrap	Used when you do not want text to wrap to window width
Blink	Text blinks on/off	Adds interest
Color	Color Color Color	Adds interest

You must highlight the text you want the character effects applied to.

Click in the margin to the left of the line or drag to select the text.

The menu equivalent is **F**ormat/**C**olor.

- Select the entire page title.

- Click [icon] Font Color.

- Select a dark red color.

- Click on the title to clear the selection.

Your screen should be similar to Figure 5-6.

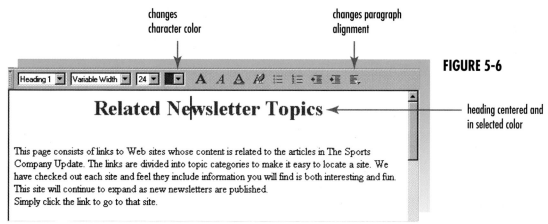

changes
character color

changes paragraph
alignment

FIGURE 5-6

heading centered and
in selected color

The title now looks much more impressive. Because the insertion point is positioned on the title, the Paragraph style, Font, Font Size, and Font Color buttons reflect the settings applied to the title.

You also want to improve the appearance of the introductory paragraph by centering it, and to add italics and bold to the newsletter name.

■ Move the insertion point to anywhere in the introductory paragraph and center it.

■ Select the newsletter title "The Sports Company Update."

■ Click **A** Bold.

■ Click **A** Italic.

■ Add bold and the same dark red color as the title to the last sentence of the introductory paragraph.

Next you want to apply heading styles and color to the two category heads Health and Fitness. Since these are the next most important headings on the page, you will apply a Heading 2 level.

■ Move the insertion point to anywhere in the word "Health" and apply a Heading 2 level.

■ Select the word "Health" and select the same dark red color as the title.

■ Apply a Heading 2 level and the same color to the word "Fitness."

■ Move to the top of the page.

> Double-click a word to select it.

> Scroll the page to see the Fitness heading.

Your screen should be similar to Figure 5-7.

FIGURE 5-7

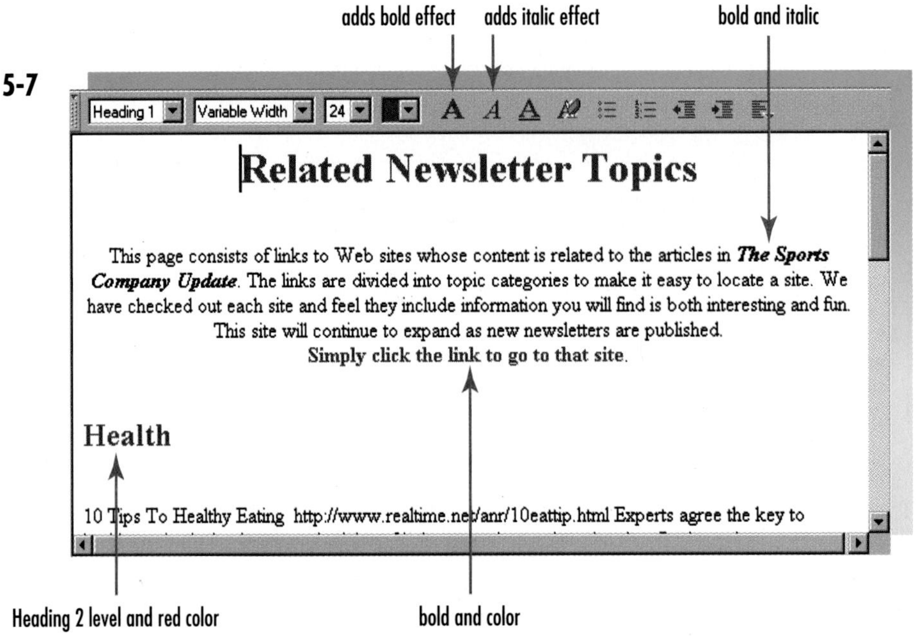

adds bold effect   adds italic effect   bold and italic

Related Newsletter Topics

This page consists of links to Web sites whose content is related to the articles in *The Sports Company Update*. The links are divided into topic categories to make it easy to locate a site. We have checked out each site and feel they include information you will find is both interesting and fun. This site will continue to expand as new newsletters are published. Simply click the link to go to that site.

Health

10 Tips To Healthy Eating http://www.realtime.net/anr/10eattip.html Experts agree the key to

Heading 2 level and red color   bold and color

Adding a Background

So far, your page is very plain and contains a lot of text. You still want to make several changes to improve the appearance of the page. One of the quickest changes you can make to enhance the appearance of the Web page is by changing the background. A **background** is a color or design that is displayed behind the text on the page. You can change the background to another color or select a background image, pattern, or texture, called a **wallpaper**. To add a background,

> Any picture image that has a bitmap file type (.bmp) can be converted for use as wallpaper.

- Choose F**o**rmat/Pa**g**e Colors and Properties.
- If necessary, open the Colors and Background tab.

The Page Properties dialog box on your screen should be similar to Figure 5-8.

FIGURE 5-8

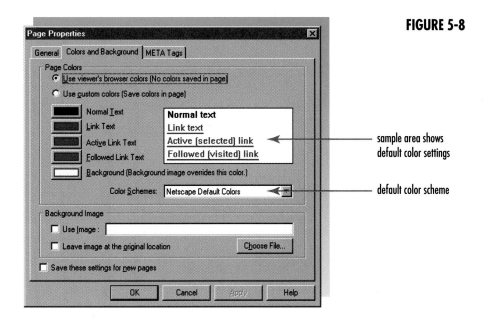

sample area shows
default color settings

default color scheme

The Colors and Background tab allows you to modify the text color of regular text as well as hyperlink text and apply a background color or wallpaper to the Web page. The current settings are Netscape's default page settings. The sample area shows the default selections for each text color with the default background of white. To try a different color scheme,

■ Open the Color Schemes drop-down list and select a color scheme of your choice.

The sample area shows how your selection will look. To see how this setting will actually look on the page,

■ Click ▭Apply▭.

Your screen should be similar to Figure 5-9.

FIGURE 5-9

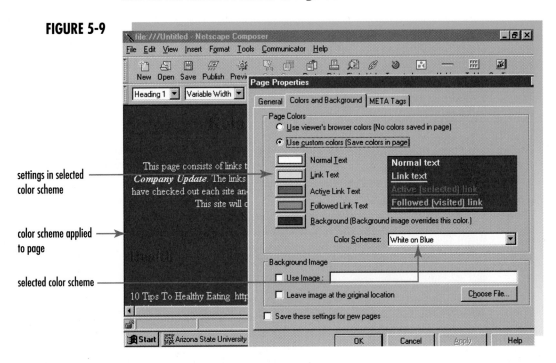

settings in selected
color scheme

color scheme applied
to page

selected color scheme

Move the dialog box to the side to
better view the page.

This figure shows the white on blue
color scheme.

The color scheme settings you selected are applied to the page, and the dialog box remains open so you can make other selections if you are not happy with your choice. Next, you will try a background wallpaper instead. The image you will use for your wallpaper is on your data disk.

- Select Use Image.

- Click Choose File... .

- From the Choose Image File dialog box, set the Look In location to the drive containing your data disk.

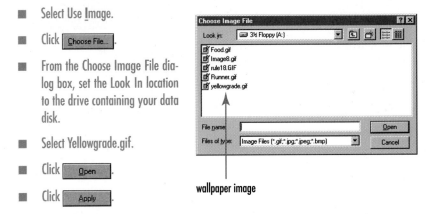

wallpaper image

- Select Yellowgrade.gif.

- Click Open .

- Click Apply .

The background image you selected overlays much of the background color of your selected color scheme. The text colors, however, are not changed.

- Return the color scheme to the Netscape Default Colors Setting.

- Click Apply .

- Click OK .

Your screen should be similar to Figure 5-10.

FIGURE 5-10

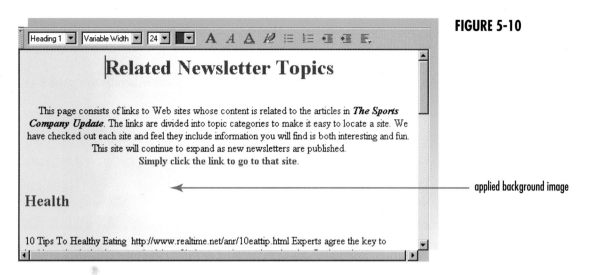

applied background image

Inserting Images

Next to each of the category heads, you want to display the same pictures that are in the newsletter. Picture images and other types of graphic objects are one of the most important features of the Web pages.

Concept 6: Images

Authors use images in Web pages to provide information or decoration, or to communicate their personal or organizational style. They are also commonly used to display graphic artwork or pictures of products for sale. Each graphic item you insert in an HTML file is stored in a separate file that is accessed and loaded by the browser at the same time as the page is loaded. Composer creates a link to the object's file in the HTML file. The link is a tag that includes the location and file name of the object the browser is to load and display in the page.

Graphic objects are commonly inserted into HTML documents in GIF and JPEG file formats. (JPEG files use the file name extension .jpg.)

If you insert an image that is not in either of these formats, the image will be saved in the GIF format when the file is saved.

Another feature associated with graphic objects is how text aligns with the object or wraps around the object. You can specify whether to have the image right-align or left-align on the page. You can also specify the particular sides you want the text to wrap to and the distance between the object and the text that surrounds it. The five alignment and two wrapping styles are shown below.

Top (even with top of line text)

Bottom (even with bottom line of text)

Right (text wraps left around image)

Center (center on line without text)

Bottom (even with bottom of lowest character on line of text)

Center (with bottom of line of type)

Left (text wraps to right around image)

Many Web pages use a table layout to gain greater control over paragraph alignment and image placement.

First you will add the picture of food before the Health heading.

■ Move to the beginning of the word "Health."

■ Click 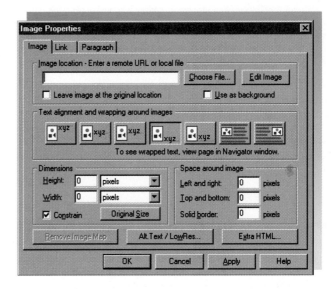.

The Image Properties dialog box on your screen should be similar to Figure 5-11.

FIGURE 5-11

This dialog box is used to insert a new image or modify an existing image's properties, such as text wrapping, height and width, and spacing. To specify a picture image to insert,

■ Click Choose File... .

■ Change the location to your data disk and select the picture file Food.gif.

■ Click Open .

■ Click OK .

The picture is inserted, but it is much too large and you would like to reduce its size. To do this you must first select the object.

■ Click on the food picture.

The menu equivalent is Insert/Image.

You screen should be similar to Figure 5-12.

inserts pictures

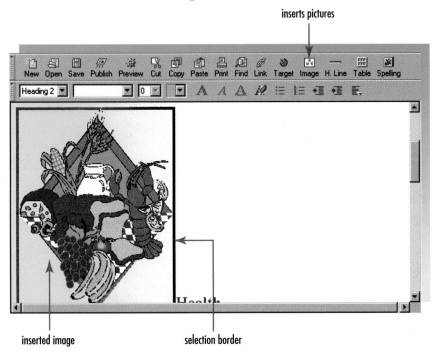

FIGURE 5-12

inserted image   selection border

A border surrounds the picture, indicating it is selected and can now be sized and moved. A graphic object is sized much like you size a window. You want to reduce the image to approximately 1.5 inches wide by 2 inches high.

- Point to the lower right corner of the selected image.

- When the mouse pointer is ↖, drag the mouse inward to reduce the size of the picture to approximately 1.5 by 2 inches.

Your screen should be similar to Figure 5-13.

> The mouse pointer changes to ↖, just as it does when resizing a window.

> Dragging a corner handle maintains the original proportions of the picture.

> When the mouse pointer is 👆, this indicates you will move the graphic when you drag the mouse.

FIGURE 5-13

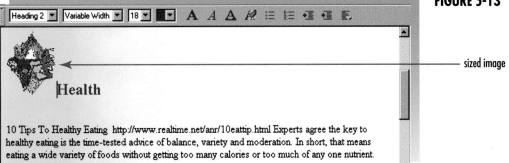

sized image

You also want to change how the text wraps around the image. To change the properties associated with this picture,

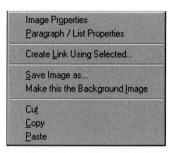

- Right-click the image.

- Select Image Properties from the pop-up menu.

- Click [icon] Wrap Right.

- Click [OK].

The change in wrapping style cannot be seen in the Composer window. You will see the change when you preview the page in the Navigator window shortly.

- In a similar manner, insert the image Runner.gif before the Fitness heading. Set the wrapping to Right and size it as in Figure 5-14.

Your screen should be similar to Figure 5-14.

FIGURE 5-14

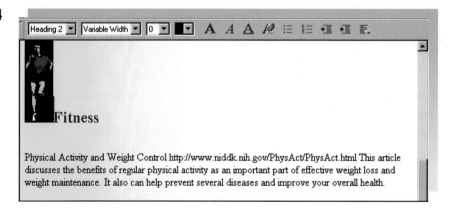

Previewing the Page

To see how your page will look when displayed in the Navigator window, you can preview it.

The menu equivalent is **F**ile/**B**rowse Page.

- Click [Preview].

An informational box is displayed advising you that you must save the new Web page to a file before you can preview it. Composer automatically saves all Web pages you create as HTML files (.html). To do this,

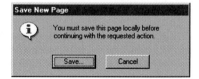

- Click [Save...].

- If a second dialog box appears asking if you want to save changes to this file, click [Yes].

- In the Save As dialog box, change the location to the drive containing your data disk.

- Enter the file name of Newsletter Links.

- Click [Save].

Next the Page Title dialog box is displayed in which you enter a title for the page. Each page includes a title that is displayed in the browser window title bar when the page is displayed. The information in the title is used by most Web search tools to locate specific Web pages. It is also used as the page's bookmark title. You will replace the current path and file name with a more descriptive title.

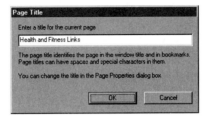

- Enter **Health and Fitness Links** as the page title.

- Click [OK].

Your screen should be similar to Figure 5-15.

page title

FIGURE 5-15

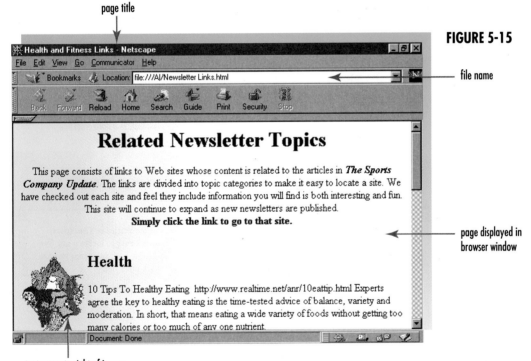

file name

page displayed in browser window

text wraps to right of image

The page is displayed in the Navigator window. The Composer window is still open behind the Navigator window. Now you can see that the text wraps to the right of the pictures.

- Scroll the page to see the Fitness area of topics.

The page is much more interesting with the addition of the graphics. You still want to add lines, bullets, and other enhancements to improve its appearance.

- Click 🖉.

Adding Rules

Next you want to separate the introductory paragraph from the Health section of the page with a horizontal line or rule.

The menu equivalent is Insert/ Horizontal Line.

■   Move to the blank line above the food image.

■   Click [H. Line].

A simple gray rule is inserted across the width of the page. You decide this is not very interesting and instead want to insert a more interesting rule. To delete the rule and insert another rule,

■   Press [Backspace].

■   Click [Image].

■   Click [Choose File...].

■   Select the picture file Rule18.gif.

■   Click [Open].

■   Click [OK].

Your screen should be similar to Figure 5-16.

FIGURE 5-16

creates a horizontal line

horizontal rule ⟶

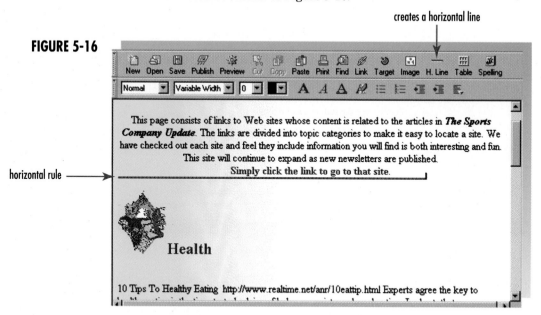

This is a moving horizontal rule that adds interest and animation to the page. However, it is a little too short.

■   Point to the right end of the rule and when the mouse pointer is a ↗, drag to the right until the rule is even with the introductory paragraph's right margin.

Creating a Bulleted List

Next you want to add bullets to the beginning of each link description in the list.

- Move to the first Web page description under Health.

- Click 📇 Bullet List.

The menu equivalent is F**o**rmat/**L**ist/ **B**ulletted.

Click 📇 again to remove a bullet.

Your screen should be similar to Figure 5-17.

FIGURE 5-17

inserts a bullet

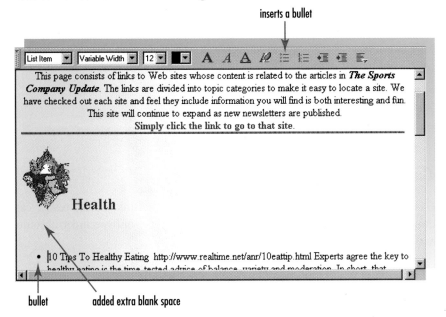

bullet   added extra blank space

A plain circular bullet is added to the first line of the description, and the entire paragraph is indented. In addition, this style inserts extra space around each bulleted list item.

- Add bullets to each of the seven remaining page descriptions.

You would like to preview how your changes look again. Each time you want to preview your changes, you need to first save the Web page file. In addition, because the Navigator preview window is already open, you can simply switch to the window.

- Click 💾 Save.
- Switch to the Navigator preview window.

Click 🏃 Health and Fitness Links... in the taskbar.

The Navigator window still displays the original page. To see the changes you have made,

- Click ↻ Reload.

This instructs the browser to reload the same file and display it with the new changes that have been made.

Your screen should be similar to Figure 5-18.

FIGURE 5-18

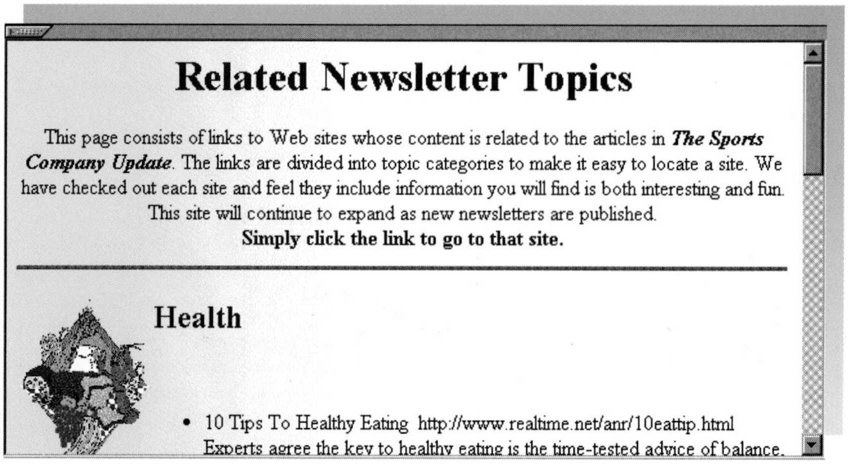

Related Newsletter Topics

This page consists of links to Web sites whose content is related to the articles in *The Sports Company Update*. The links are divided into topic categories to make it easy to locate a site. We have checked out each site and feel they include information you will find is both interesting and fun. This site will continue to expand as new newsletters are published.
Simply click the link to go to that site.

Health

- 10 Tips To Healthy Eating http://www.realtime.net/anr/10eattip.html
Experts agree the key to healthy eating is the time-tested advice of balance.

Creating Links

Next, you want to convert the site references to hyperlinks so the reader can quickly jump to the associated site. There are two types of hyperlinks, absolute and relative.

Concept 7: Absolute and Relative Links

When you create a hyperlink in a Web page, you can make the path to the destination of the hyperlink an absolute link or a relative link. An **absolute link**, also called a **fixed link**, is a link that identifies the file location of the destination by its full address, such as c:/Word Data File/Sales.doc. A **relative link** identifies the destination location in relation to the location of the Web page file. A relative link is based on a path you specify in which the first part of the path is shared by both the Web page file that contains the hyperlink and the destination file.

Relative links change when the Web page file is moved to another location. They are used to make it easy to copy materials to another location, which is needed for example, when you upload your Web pages to a server. A fixed link will not change, regardless if you move the Web page file to another location. Fixed links are usually only used if you are sure the location of the destination file will not change. Hyperlinks to documents on other Web sites are called **external links** and should typically use a fixed file location that includes the URL of the page.

You will change the name of each site to a hyperlink. Since the sites are external links, they require the use of an absolute link address. You will use the URL in each description to create the link.

■ Display the Composer window.

■ Select the URL following the text "10 Tips To Healthy Eating" in the first site description.

■ Click [Cut] to remove it from the page and store it in the Clipboard.

■ Select the text "10 Tips To Healthy Eating."

■ Click [Link].

The Character Properties dialog box on your screen should be similar to Figure 5-19.

The menu equivalent is Insert/Link, and the keyboard shortcut is Ctrl + ⇧Shift + L.

FIGURE 5-19

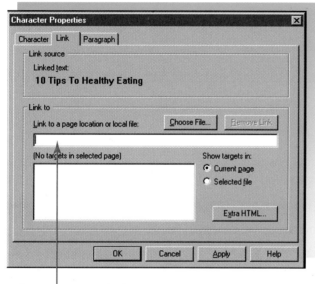

enter URL to document on an external Web site

In the Link tab you enter the URL for the link you are creating. To paste the URL from the Clipboard into the Link to a Page Location text box, you will need to use the keyboard shortcut for the Paste command.

■ Press Ctrl + V.

■ Click [OK].

■ Click the page to clear the selection.

Your screen should be similar to Figure 5-20.

creates a hypertext link

FIGURE 5-20

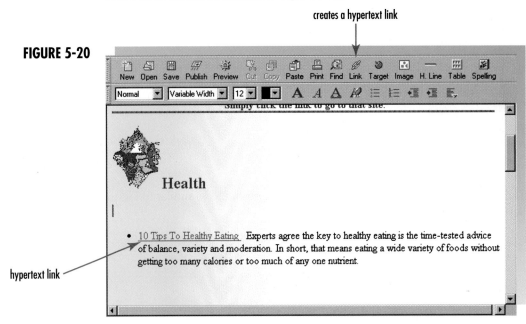

hypertext link

The selected text appears formatted as a hypertext link.

The hyperlink color may vary from one browser to another.

■ In the same manner, cut the URLs for each description and create a link to the description title.

Move to the blank line and press [Backspace].

■ Delete the extra blank lines between link descriptions and below the two category headings.

■ Save the page and preview your changes.

This page should also include links to other pages within The Sports Company Web site. Because you do not know the locations of those pages, you will leave it to the Web site administrator to add those links. However, you do want to include a link at the bottom of the page to quickly return to the top of the page. To do this you create a **target** or **anchor** in the document and then create a link that points to the target. When you click on the link, the browser scrolls to the target location. First you will create the target.

The target can be in the current page or another page in the Web site.

■ Switch to the Composer window.

■ Move the insertion point to the beginning of the page title.

The menu equivalent is <u>I</u>nsert/<u>T</u>arget.

■ Click [Target].

A target name can be up to 30 characters long.

■ Enter the name **Top of page** for the target in the Target Properties box.

■ Click [OK].

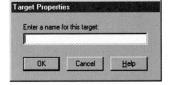

Your screen should be similar to Figure 5-21.

target icon marks location of target   creates a target

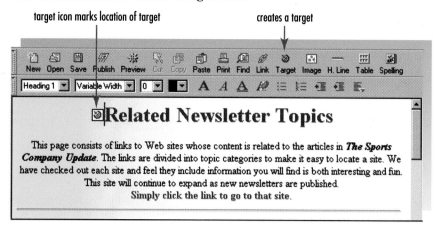

FIGURE 5-21

A special target icon ▩ appears in the document to mark the location of the target. Next you need to enter the text for the link at the bottom of the page and create the link to the target.

> The target icon is visible only in the Composer window.

   ■   Type the text **Top of Page** at the bottom of the page.

   ■   Press ⎵Enter.

   ■   Select the Top of Page text.

   ■   Click ⬚Link.

The Character Properties dialog box on your screen should be similar to Figure 5-22.

FIGURE 5-22

selected text

targets in current page

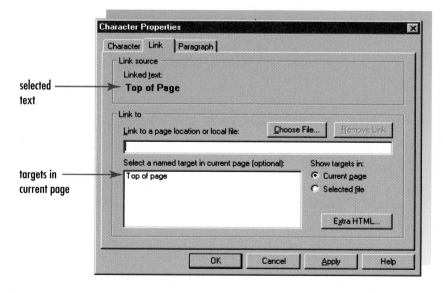

The name of the target you created is displayed in the list box. Next you will select the target as the location to link to and see if your target link works correctly.

■ Select Top of Page in the list box.

■ Click [OK] .

■ Click [Preview] .

■ Click [Yes] .

■ Click the <u>Top of Page</u> link.

The top of the page where the anchor is located is displayed in the window. Next you will go online to check the other links.

■ Click <u>10 Tips to Healthy Eating</u>.

■ If your computer displays the screen to access your Internet provider, enter the requested user identification.

> The mouse pointer changes to hand over a hyperlink, and the URL appears in the status bar.

Navigator locates the Web page, loads it, and displays it in the window.
Your screen should be similar to Figure 5-23.

FIGURE 5-23

To return to the Newsletter Links page,

■ Click [Back] .

■ Close the Navigator window and disconnect from the Internet.

Your Web page should be displayed in Composer.

■ Display the HTML source code.

Use **V**iew/Page So**u**rce.

Your screen should be similar to Figure 5-24.

FIGURE 5-24

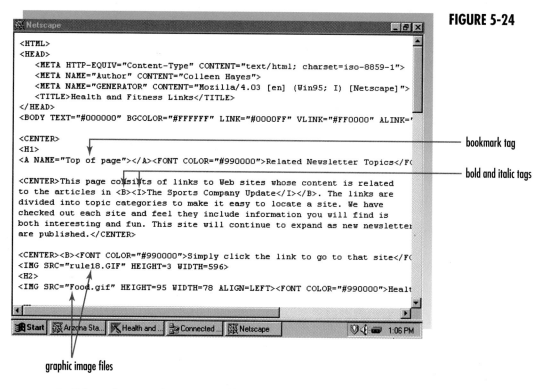

bookmark tag

bold and italic tags

graphic image files

■ Scroll the window to see the entire HTML file.

As you can see, many more HTML tags have been added to the file. Notice that each graphic element you inserted into the page has been saved as separate image files with .gif file extensions.

■ Close the Page Source window.

■ Add your name and the current date at the bottom of the Web page. Save the Web page.

■ Choose **F**ile/Print Pre**v**iew to preview how the page will appear when printed.

■ Make any necessary adjustments to fit the Web page on a single printed page, then print the page.

Publishing Your Page

The process of placing your Web pages on a server for public access by others is commonly referred to as **publishing**. Before making your Web page public, however, you should test that all links work correctly. In addition, because all browsers do not display the HTML tags the same way, it is a good idea to preview your page using different browsers. Many of the differences in how browsers display a page are appearance differences, not structural.

How do you get your page on the Internet so others can see it? The steps that you take to make your pages available to other people depend on how you want to share them. There are two main avenues: on your local network or intranet server for limited access by people within an organization, or on an Internet server for access by anyone using the WWW. In either case, you need to upload your Web page files and all related files, such as pictures and rules, to a remote server. If you do not include all the files, your links will not work. You should ask the Web administrator how the Web pages, graphics files, and other files should be structured on the server. For instance, find out whether you need to create separate folders for bullets and pictures, or whether you need to store all the files in one location. If you plan to use forms or image maps, you should ask about any limitations on using these items, because they require additional server support.

You can use FTP to transfer the files to the server, or you can use the File/Publish command or the ⊞Publish button in Composer. Using the Publish command makes the process quick and easy. The program simply asks you to select the files or directories you want to upload (publish) to a remote server and the location of the server.

■ Save the Web page and exit Composer.

> Refer to the Appendix for more information on FTP.

> To make your Web pages available on the WWW, you need to either install Web server software on your computer or locate an Internet service provider that allocates space for Web pages.

LAB REVIEW

■ ■ ■ ■ ■ ■ ■ ■ ■ ■ ■

Key Terms

absolute link (NET168)
alignment (NET155)
anchor (NET170)
author (NET148)
background (NET158)
Composer (NET147)
external link (NET168)
fixed (NET154)
fixed link (NET168)
font (NET154)
point (NET154)
publish (NET173)
relative link (NET168)
tag (NET150)
target (NET170)
typeface (NET154)
variable (NET154)
wallpaper (NET158)

Command Summary

Command	Shortcut Key	Button	Action
File/**Pu**blish		Publish	Uploads current file to a server
File/**B**rowse Page		Preview	Displays page in Navigator window
View/Page So**u**rce			Displays HTML code of current page
Insert/**L**ink	Ctrl + ⇧ Shift + L	Link	Creates a hypertext link
Insert/**Ta**rget		Target	Creates an anchor
Insert/**I**mage		Image	Adds an image to a page
Insert/**H**orizontal Line		H. Line	Inserts horizontal line across page
F**o**rmat/**C**olor		▮▾	Changes text color
F**o**rmat/**H**eading		Normal ▾	Applies a predefined paragraph style
F**o**rmat/**L**ist/**B**ulletted			Creates bulleted list of selected text
F**o**rmat/**A**lign			Changes position of lines between margins
F**o**rmat/Pa**g**e Colors and Properties			Changes color of text and background

Matching

1. Preview _____
2. font _____
3. external link _____
4. _____
5. tags _____
6. alignment _____
7. wallpaper _____
8. images _____
9. authoring _____
10. absolute link _____

  a. how text is positioned between margins
  b. creates bulleted list of selected text
  c. identifies file location by its full address
  d. displayed behind text on a Web page
  e. hyperlink to a document on another Web site
  f. embedded codes that supply information about Web page
  g. used to personalize and enhance a Web page
  h. creating a Web page
  i. previews Web page in browser
  j. set of character typefaces

Fill-In Questions

1. Complete the following statements by filling in the blanks with the correct terms.

   a. _____ and _____ are elements that can be added to a Web page to make it attractive and easy to use.

   b. Embedded codes that supply information about the Web page's structure, appearance, and contents are called _____.

   c. A _____ is a specific character design.

   d. _____ can be applied to text to add emphasis or interest to a page.

   e. A _____ is used to create a link to a location in your Web site.

   f. Links to a Web page outside your Web site are _____ links.

   g. A _____ is displayed behind the text to enhance the appearance of a page.

   h. Viewing the page source displays the _____ of the current page.

   i. To _____ a Web page means to upload it to a server for access by the public.

   j. Unless otherwise specified, Web images are saved in _____ format.

Discussion Questions

1. Discuss three attributes of a well-designed Web page.

2. Discuss how images are saved in an HTML document.

3. Discuss the two types of hyperlinks and when they would be used.

4. Discuss how to get your Web page on the Internet.

Hands-On Practice Exercises

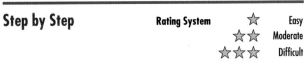

Step by Step	Rating System	☆	Easy
		☆☆	Moderate
		☆☆☆	Difficult

1. Netscape provides a set of Web page templates with which to create your own custom Web pages. You will use one of these templates to create a Web page for a business of your choice.

   a. Start Communicator and from the File menu, choose New/Page from Template Netscape templates.

   b. Read the explanation on how to use a template.

   c. Choose one of the business templates and modify it using the features you learned in the lab to create a business of your choice.

   d. You can use the search tools you learned about in earlier labs to find pictures and graphics to use on your page. (Remember that many pictures are copyright protected so don't publish your page without getting permission from the owner.)

   e. Print your final Web page.

2. Another way to create Web pages is to use the page design Wizard to guide you step by step through the process. You will use these feature to create a simple Web page.

   a. Start Communicator and choose File/New/Page from Wizard.

   b. Read the directions on how to use the wizard and click Start to begin.

   c. Follow the instructions and create a Web page that contains information about a club or organization that you belong to.

   d. Add any editing and formatting changes to the page.

   e. Print your final Web page.

3. In this problem you will create a personal home page.

a. Plan the design of your home page. You may want to visit other personal home pages on the Web to get an idea of what you like and do not like for your page.

b. Develop the text of your home page and type it directly into the Composer window.

c. Add appropriate paragraph and character formatting.

d. Add a background.

e. Add rules, pictures, and animation to your home page.

f. Create links to other Web pages that are of interest to you.

g. If possible, publish your home page to a server so others may enjoy your work.

h. Print your home page.

4. Andrew Beinbrink has asked you to help him create a Web page for Call Animation Studio. This studio helps independent graphic designers promote their animated drawings.

a. Design a home page for the Call Animation Studio.

b. Include appropriate paragraph and character formatting.

c. Add a background, rules, and pictures of animation characters to the page to add interest.

d. Create a second page that includes links to Web pages containing information about computer animation.

e. Format the second page appropriately.

f. Add links on both pages to access the other page.

g. Print the pages you created.

■ ■ ■ ■ ■ ■ ■ ■ ■ □ □ □

Creating Web Pages

Web Page Design

There are many elements that can be added to a Web page to make it attractive and easy to use. Graphic objects, images, art, and color are perhaps the most important features of Web pages.

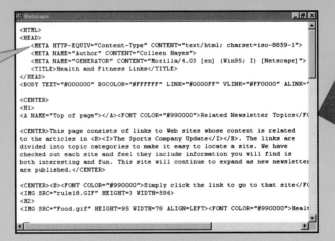

HTML Tags

HTML tags are embedded codes that supply information about the page's structure, appearance, and contents.

Absolute and Relative Links

When you create a hyperlink in a Web page, you can make the path to the destination of the hyperlink an absolute link or a relative link.

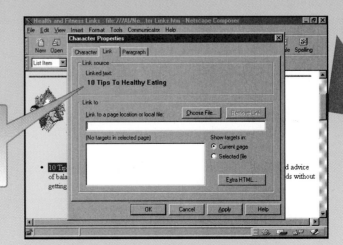

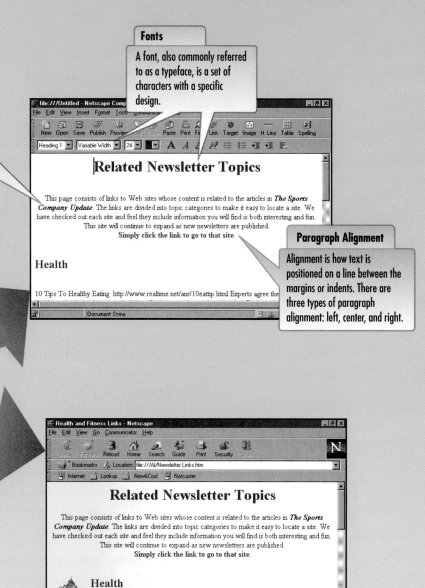

Fonts

A font, also commonly referred to as a typeface, is a set of characters with a specific design.

Character Effects

Different character effects such as bold, italics, and color can be applied to selections to add emphasis or interest to a page.

Paragraph Alignment

Alignment is how text is positioned on a line between the margins or indents. There are three types of paragraph alignment: left, center, and right.

Concepts

Web Page Design

HTML Tags

Fonts
Paragraph Alignment
Character Effects

Images

Absolute and Relative Links

Images

Authors use images in Web pages to provide information or decoration, or to communicate their personal or organizational style.

Appendix

Additional Internet Tools: FTP, Telnet, and Gopher

As the Internet has developed, some programs, such as Gopher, that were initially used to access information on the Internet have been replaced by new programs and procedures. Others, such as FTP, have become an integral part of the browser programs. However, in your travels over the Internet you will still come across these programs and will need to understand them and in some cases know how to use them to access information.

File Transfer Protocol

Using Netscape Communicator, you have viewed Web pages that are downloaded to your computer and can be saved as files to a disk. These links begin with HTTP, indicating the protocol that is used to transfer the file. Many other files that you will encounter, such as software applications, graphic images, or very large text files, cannot be viewed by Netscape but can only be downloaded and saved to your disk. These links commonly begin with **FTP**, indicating that the protocol used to transfer files between computers is the File Transfer Protocol and that the files are stored on FTP servers rather than HTTP servers.

FTP sites, called archives or repositories, are located on computers throughout the Internet. Many sites are public, meaning anyone can download the files contained on the site to their computer. They may require a password, usually the word "anonymous," before access is granted. For that reason these sites are commonly called anonymous FTP archive sites. FTP sites are usually text based with minimal formatting and appear as a hierarchy of directories/folders and files.

One of the main reasons for the need to download files using FTP is the incorporation of complicated animation, audio, movies, and 3-D virtual reality in Web pages. Although Netscape can display many of these types of files, it is often necessary to obtain special viewer or software enhancement applications to display them. Many of these files can be obtained from the Internet and installed on your computer to run in conjunction with Netscape. They are commonly divided into two categories: shareware and freeware. **Shareware** are software programs you can try before buying. If you like it, a fee is requested for using it. When you pay and register as a licensed user, you are informed of upgrades as they happen. **Freeware**, also called public domain software, are programs that are available on the Internet without a fee for use. Many freeware programs are used to enhance Navigator's ability to view or play media files. These include plug-ins and helper applications.

Plug-ins are applications that supplement the capabilities of Communicator. Plug-in tools automatically detect the non-HTML components of a page, such as sound or video, and automatically load and run while you are viewing the page. Many plug-ins are automatically installed with Communicator, such as Apple's Quicktime video that plays movie files with .qt, .mov, and .moov file extensions. Others, however, can be downloaded and added to the Communicator plug-in folder. Some common plug-in tools are listed in the table below.

Plug-in	Runs: File Extension
Live3D, Community Place, WIRL 1.2	Virtual reality: .wrl
MidPlug, Live Audio, VivoActive	Sound: .au, .aiff, .wav, .midi
LiveVideo	Microsoft video: .avi
Bamba (IBM)	Audio-video streaming: .ra, .rv

Streaming programs allow an audio or video file to be played while the file is downloading.

Helper applications (also commonly referred to as helper apps) are standalone programs that play sound and video files. Helper applications expand Communicator's ability to interpret and display different kinds of files that the standard plug-ins cannot. Once a helper app is installed on your system and you show Communicator where it is located, it will load automatically when needed to run a file. To keep track of the file formats requiring helper applications, Communicator maintains a mapping between file formats and helper applications. When Communicator retrieves a file with a format that Communicator itself cannot read, the application looks at the mapping to find the appropriate application capable of handling the file format. Some helper applications are described in the table on the next page.

Because plug-ins operate seamlessly within Navigator, they are often preferred to helper apps. Many helper applications are being converted to plug-ins. If you have the choice, download a plug-in instead of a helper app.

Helper App	Runs
Decompression	
PKZip	Compresses and decompresses files.
WinZip	Compresses and decompresses files.
Animation	
Shockwave www.macromedia.com/ shockwave	Plays files created in Macromedia Director, a popular animation creation and authoring tool.
Enliven www.enliven.com	Converts Director movies into streaming files that start to play after a short buffer period.
Streaming Audio	
RealPlayer www.realaudio.com	Combines superior audio quality with streaming video.
TrueSpeech www.dspg.com	High-quality audio.
Liquid MusicPlayer www.liquidaudio.com	Used to sample music over the net.
Streaming Video	
VivoActive www.vivo.com	Non-scalable streaming video.

Although there are special FTP programs that you can use to transfer files, Netscape Communicator has very conveniently included this feature in Navigator. Navigator lets you access FTP servers in the same way you access World Wide Web (HTTP) servers. It handles the interface to the FTP server and the entry of the password automatically for you. On the surface, downloading an FTP file using Navigator appears no different than saving a Web page or image you are viewing. You can also upload files to a site on another computer; however, you must have permission to upload from the site first.

The procedure to download FTP files is the same regardless of whether the file is text, video, audio, or image. The following four steps describe this procedure.

1. Locate the file to download.

   ■ Use a specialized FTP search engine such as Archie, which indexes FTP sites throughout the Internet. Filez, FTPSearch95, Snoopie, Jumbo, Shareware.com, and Download.com are other sources.

   ■ Alternatively, you can go directly to an FTP server by typing the FTP URL in the Location field.

2. Click on the link to the name of the file you want to download. This starts the procedure to download and save the file.

3. After a file is downloaded, you may need to expand it using a decompression program on your computer before you can use it. Most large files you download will be compressed (zipped) files. Compression programs shrink files so that they are smaller and thereby quicker to transfer between computers. Then you decompress (unzip) the file to expand it before using it. Some compressed files are self-extracting, meaning they uncompress automatically when opened.

4. If the file is a software program, install the program, then run it. If it is a text, video, or audio file, open the file to view or hear the content using the appropriate type of program, such as a word processor for text or a sound or video helper application for audio or movies.

Using FTP

C/Net's Shareware.com site is a great place to locate software to download. It breaks the index of FTP files into categories for quicker search retrieval. Or you can type in a keyword to search on if you know the name of the item you want to download. It also includes a Most Popular category and a New Arrivals category. You will use this site to download a screen saver program—a program that displays animated pictures on your screen after a period of inactivity.

Netscape maintains its own FTP site for downloading plug-in and helper application software. Choose **H**elp/**S**oftware Updates or Abou**t** Plug-ins to access these files.

   ■ If necessary, start Netscape Communicator and establish your Internet connection.

   ■ Type **shareware.com** in the Location text box.

   ■ Press ←Enter.

Your screen should be similar to Figure A-1.

FIGURE A-1

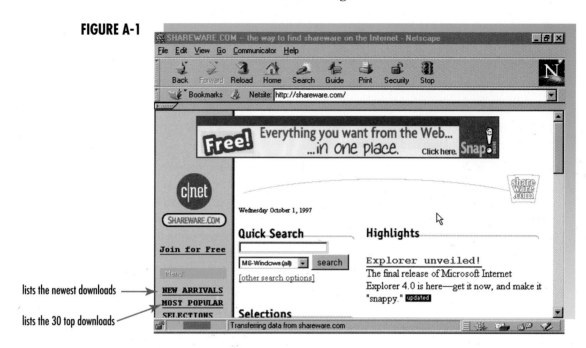

lists the newest downloads ⟶

lists the 30 top downloads ⟶

■ Type **screen saver** in the Quick Search text box.

■ Click search .

Your screen should be similar to Figure A-2.

FIGURE A-2

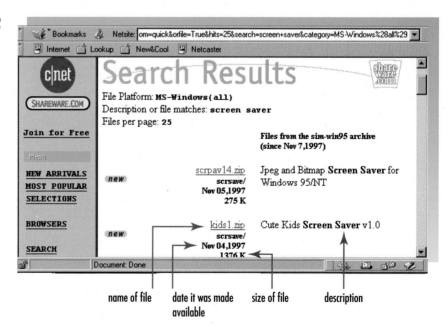

name of file   date it was made
                available
size of file   description

A list of screen saver files is displayed. It includes a brief description of the file, the date it was made available, and the file size. The files are listed in date order. You will select a file to download to your data disk. When you select a file, note the size of the file.

■ Click on any screen saver file link that is of interest to you.

Your screen should be similar to Figure A-3.

reliability rating of site   available FTP sites categorized by country

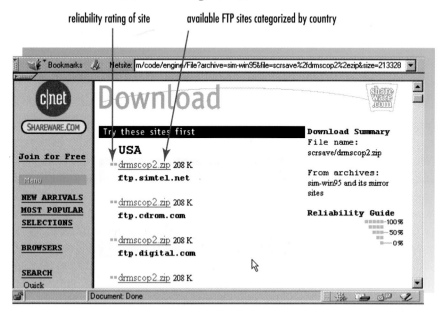

FIGURE A-3

This window lists the sites from which you can download the file. Popular files are often located on more than one machine. These multiple sites are called "mirror" sites. The sites are listed in order of reliability and are categorized by country. It is suggested that you use the first listed site that is close to your location so that the transfer is as fast as possible.

■ Click on a link to an appropriate site for your location.

■ Click [OK] in response to the security warning.

■ Insert a disk in the appropriate drive for your system.

■ In the Save As dialog box, change the location to the drive containing your data disk.

■ Click [Save] to save the file to your data disk using the default file name.

As the transfer is made, the progress bar in the Saving Location dialog box shows the degree of completion. If a transfer is taking too long, you can click [Cancel] to halt the transfer at any time.

■ After the file download is complete, check the size of the file to verify that the downloaded file on your disk is the same size as the original file. If not, try again.

■ If you are not continuing, exit Netscape Communicator and disconnect from the Internet.

Once download is complete, you can unzip the file using an appropriate utility program such as PKZip or WinZip. Then read the read.me file that is commonly included on how to use the software and follow the directions to install or set up the program. If it is a self-extracting file, simply double-click on the file name to unzip and install it.

Telnet

Through Netscape you can also communicate directly to other computers on the Internet using Telnet. **Telnet** is an application that allows you to log on and communicate from your local personal computer to a remote computer. After logging on to a remote computer, you can run programs on that computer by typing single-line commands or by selecting from a menu.

Using Telnet

You will use Telnet to communicate with a library and search for books and information on computer crime. Why would you want to browse a library you cannot physically visit? Many libraries share books, so if yours does not have what you want, you can tell the librarian where to get it. Or if you live in an area where the libraries are not yet online, you can use Telnet to do some basic bibliographic research before you go to your local branch. Several hundred libraries around the world, including the Library of Congress, are available to you through Telnet. You will connect to the University of Minnesota library.

■ If necessary, start Netscape Communicator and establish your Internet connection.

■ In the location field type **telnet://pubinfo.ais.umn.edu**

■ Press ⎆Enter.

Your screen should be similar to Figure A-4.

type ? to display menu of options

FIGURE A-4

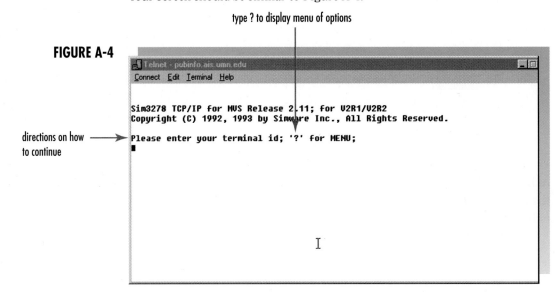

directions on how to continue

The connection is made, and a Telnet window is opened. You are now communicating directly with another computer and have established a constant connection to this computer. Information on how to proceed is displayed. You will display the menu of terminal options.

■ Type **?**

■ Press ⟨←Enter⟩.

Your screen should be similar to Figure A-5.

menu options and descriptions

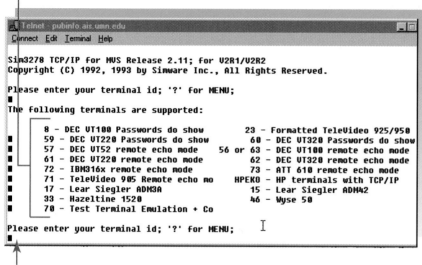

FIGURE A-5

enter option number here

The next screen lists the different terminal options as menu selections. Dec VT100 is one of the most common.

■ Type **8** (or the appropriate menu option for your system).

■ Press ⟨←Enter⟩.

If you cannot establish a Telnet connection, continue with the next section "Gopher," on page NET190.

During a Telnet session, you must press ⟨←Enter⟩ after typing your command to send it to the other computer.

If you do not see your keyboard input, choose **T**erminal/**P**references/Local **E**cho to turn on this feature.

Your screen should be similar to Figure A-6.

FIGURE A-6

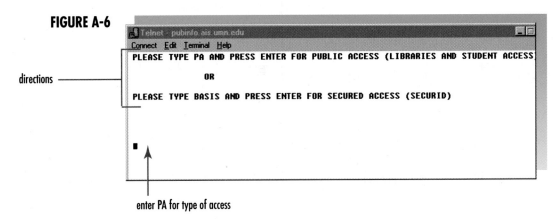

directions

enter PA for type of access

In the next window you enter the access word. Following the instructions on the screen, to enter the public access password,

■ Type **pa**

■ Press ⏎Enter.

Next you will enter a series of commands to connect with the University of Minnesota Library. Again, instructions on how to proceed are included (at the bottom of the screen). You will find that different locations you access using Telnet have different appearances and different procedures. Usually there is a Help command that provides instructions on basic navigational procedures and directions on how to exit the Telnet session.

■ Type **1** (to select University libraries).

■ Press ⏎Enter.

■ Type **mncat** (to go to the catalog).

■ Press ⏎Enter.

■ Type **go**

■ Press ⏎Enter.

Your screen should be similar to Figure A-7.

catalog menu

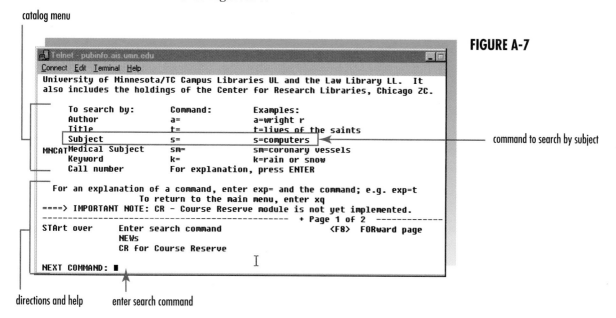

FIGURE A-7

command to search by subject

directions and help   enter search command

The main catalog menu of options is displayed. You will conduct a search to locate books on computer viruses.

- Type **s=computer viruses**

- Press ⟨←Enter⟩.

Your screen should be similar to Figure A-8.

located resources on computer viruses

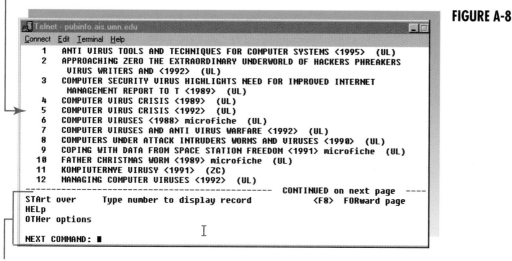

FIGURE A-8

instructions

A listing of resources containing information on the subject you requested is displayed. The total number of found resources appears at the top of the list.

■ Type a number to see more information about a listing.

■ Press ←Enter.

Your screen should be similar to Figure A-9.

FIGURE A-9

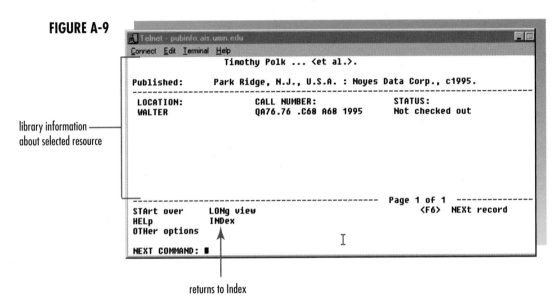

library information about selected resource

returns to Index

When you are done reading the information on your screen, to return to the index again,

■ Type **ind**

■ Press ←Enter.

■ Select other menu items to see what type of information they contain.

When you are done exploring the catalog, to quit the Telnet session,

■ Choose <u>C</u>onnect/E<u>x</u>it.

■ If you are not continuing, exit Netscape Communicator and disconnect from the Internet.

Gopher

Gopher is a program that provides a menu-based interface to allow you to search, retrieve, and display documents stored on Gopher servers. Much like FTP, Gopher has been around from the early years of the Internet. Gopher was designed at the University of Minnesota and bears the name of its mascot. Gopher was the first system that provided a menu to information stored on the Internet.

Gopher sites originally were browsed with text-line commands, such as those used with DOS. With the advent of the World Wide Web, special software was created to provide a user-friendly interface to the directories of a Gopher site.

When you log into a Gopher site, your Web browser acts as a Gopher client and displays the Gopher directory, which, like FTP, is in the form of menus and directories. These directories contain lists of hypertext documents that can be navigated through with the click of a mouse. Gopher menus are a bit more descriptive than FTP directories. For that reason the Gopher is easier to navigate than an FTP site. The information that is stored on Gopher servers and that you can access using Gopher is called **GopherSpace**.

Also like FTP, you can locate information in GopherSpace using search software. The Gopher search software is called Veronica. Using Veronica you can search by keyword or by subject area. In addition, many newer Gophers, called Gopher Jewels, are now organized by subject.

Although much of the information that is located in GopherSpace is being transferred to the World Wide Web, a large quantity of data that is still stored in Gopher format.

> Veronica is supposed to stand for Very Easy Rodent-Oriented Netwide Index to Computerized Archives.

Using Gopher

Netscape lets you access Gopher servers in the same way you access Web pages: click on a link whose URL begins with gopher or enter the URL in the Location field. You will use Veronica to locate movie information on a Gopher server about movies.

■ If necessary, start Netscape Communicator and establish your Internet connection.

■ Access Yahoo and conduct a search on the keyword **Veronica**.

■ Click Computers and Internet:Internet:Gopher:Searching:Veronica.

■ Click Veronica [unr.edu].

> You could also type gopher://veronica.scs.unr.edu:70/11/veronica in the Location field to access this Veronica server.

Your screen should be similar to Figure A-10.

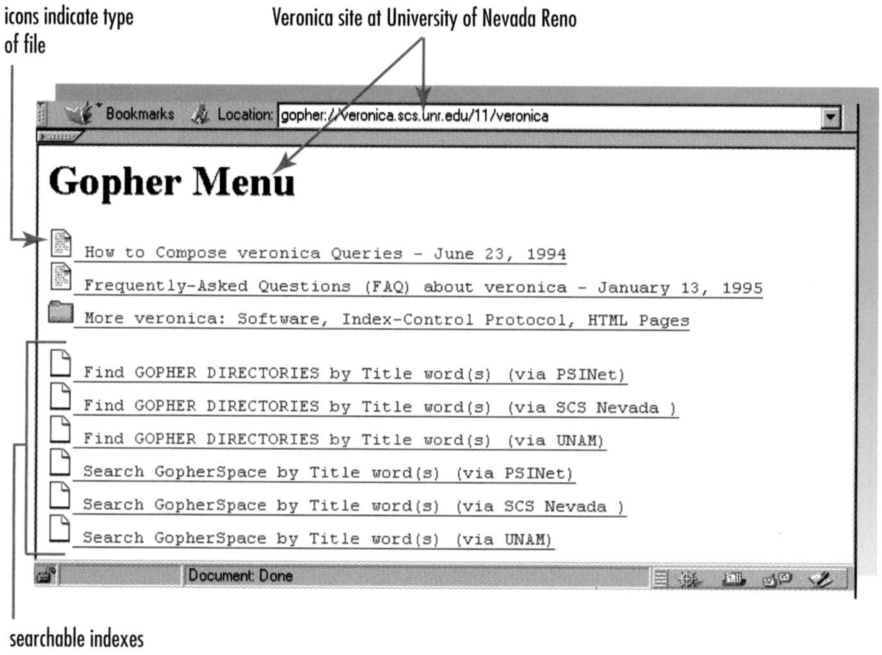

icons indicate type of file   Veronica site at University of Nevada Reno

FIGURE A-10

searchable indexes

A Gopher menu of options is displayed. The icons to left of the menu identify the type of information that will appear when you select the options. Some of the most common icons are displayed in the table below.

Icon	Meaning
	Represents a folder containing other folders or files.
	Represents a text file.
	Represents an index.
	Represents a sound file.
	Represents an image file.
	Represents a movie file.

The first two options are text files that provide information on using Veronica. The third option indicates it is a folder of resources about Veronica. The remaining options in the Gopher menu indicate they are searchable indexes. In this case they provide the means to conduct a search by presenting a search form.

You have the option of searching for words in titles of directories (folders) only or in all types of documents in GopherSpace at any of the Gopher servers listed. It does not matter which server you select, as they should all produce the same results. However, some servers may be updated more recently than others, therefore providing more up-to-date matches. Also some are more heavily used, making them slower.

■   Click <u>Find GOPHER DIRECTORIES by Title Word(s) (via SCS Nevada).</u>

Veronica site accessed

gopher://fdlpc1.scs.unr.edu:2347/7-t1
Gopher Search

This is a searchable Gopher index. Use the search function of your browser to enter search terms.

This is a searchable index. Enter search keywords: [   ]

Read the Veronica FAQ text file for more information about using Veronica.

If this option is unavailable, select any other server site.

A form appears in which you enter the text you want Veronica to locate. To locate all titles that include the words "movie" and "reviews,"

- Type **movie reviews**

- Press ←Enter.

Your screen should be similar to Figure A-11.

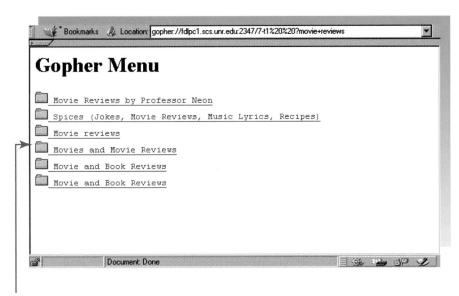

FIGURE A-11

Veronica search results

The result list displays a list of folders (directories) found in GopherSpace that contain the specified words in the title.

- Click Movie reviews.

Your screen should be similar to Figure A-12.

FIGURE A-12

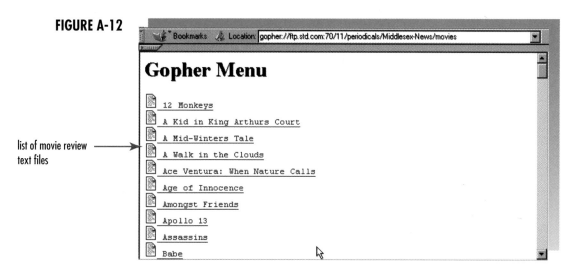

list of movie review
text files

This folder contains a list of movie review text files. Menu options preceded by 🖹 indicate selecting the item will load and display a text file.

■ Click any movie review preceded with a 🖹.

Your screen should be similar to Figure A-13.

FIGURE A-13

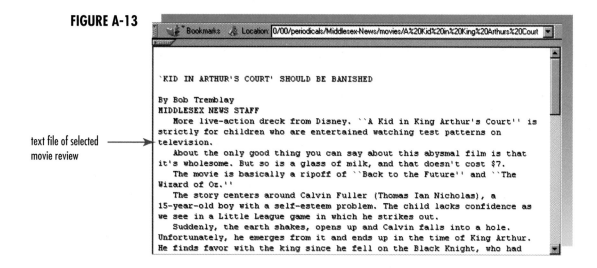

text file of selected
movie review

■ If necessary, scroll the window to read the entire document.

■ Click Back to return to the list of movie reviews.

■ When you have read as many reviews as you like, exit Netscape Communicator and disconnect from the Internet.

LAB REVIEW
■ ■ ■ ■ ■ ■ ■ ■ ■ ■ ■

Key Terms

freeware (NET181)	helper application (NET181)
FTP (NET180)	plug-in (NET181)
Gopher (NET190)	shareware (NET181)
GopherSpace (NET191)	Telnet (NET186)

Matching

1. GopherSpace _____ **a.** an FTP site

2. shareware _____ **b.** software programs you can try before buying

3. freeware _____ **c.** software programs that supplement Communicator

4. Telnet _____ **d.** the information you can access with Gopher

5. Veronica _____ **e.** used to download and upload files

6. archive _____ **f.** a program used to search GopherSpace

7. plug-in _____ **g.** stand-alone programs that play sound and video

8. FTP _____ **h.** programs available on the Internet without a fee

9. Archie _____ **i.** used to communicate directly with a remote computer

10. helper app _____ **j.** a program used to search FTP sites

Discussion Questions

1. What is FTP? What is Archie?

2. What does Telnet allow you to do?

3. What is Gopher? What is Veronica?

Hands-On Practice Exercises

Step-By-Step	Rating System	☆	Easy
		☆☆	Moderate
		☆☆☆	Difficult

1. Locate a software program of interest to you and download it to your data disk. Check the size of the file before you download it to ensure you have enough disk space.

2. Justin is doing a report on the U.S. Senate. Use Veronica to locate the FAQ file of questions people ask about the Senate.

3. Telnet to the Oxford University library (telnet:// 129.67.1.46) and search for a book in the All Soul's College using the author's name.

4. Telnet to the IRS (telnet://iris.irs.ustreas.gov) and see what information they have available. How up to date is this information? Do they have a WWW site?

5. Use Veronica to search for weather satellite images. What steps did you use to locate this information? What site(s) did you locate?

6. There are thousands of searches you could do using Veronica. Try some of the searches suggested below and then try some of your own.

   a. Do you want to find museums that might have online displays from their exhibits? Try searching for "museum" using Veronica.

   b. Are you looking for a copy of the Declaration of Independence? Try "declaration."

   c. For copies of Environmental Protection Agency fact sheets on hundreds of chemicals, try "Education" and "Environmental fact sheets."

7. You are preparing a paper for a course in your field of study. Use Veronica to locate three text files that contain information on the topic of your paper. Write down the text file names as they appear in the menu and write a brief summary of the information in the text files. Remember, you can download the files to your disk. Check the size of the file before you download it to ensure you have enough disk space.

Glossary of Key Terms

Absolute link: A link that identifies the file location of the destination by its full address. Also called a fixed link.

Address book: A file that contains a collection of names and e-mail addresses that you use frequently.

Alias: A shortcut for URLs or e-mail addresses.

Alignment: How text is positioned on a line between the margins or indents.

Anchor: A marked location within a Web site to which you can create a link. Also called a target.

Archive: To save e-mail messages.

Article: A message posted to a newsgroup.

Attachment: A text or graphic file that is attached to an e-mail message.

Author: To create a Web page.

Background: A color or design that is displayed behind the content of a Web page.

Bookmark: Permanently stores the URL of a page so that you can easily retrieve the page again.

Boolean operator: The logical operators AND, OR, and NOT that indicate a relationship among the keywords in your search.

Browser: A program used to access and display WWW pages, to access FTP sites, and to provide an interface to the Internet and WWW documents.

Cache: An area on your computer system where copies of Web pages are stored when they are downloaded.

Certificate: A tamper-resistant file used for security purposes that identifies the individual to whom it is issued and includes public and private keys.

Channel: An area where chat discussions are displayed.

Chat group: A method of communication over the Internet that allows people to converse in real time.

Collabra: Netscape Communicator's component that is used to access and read newsgroups.

Composer: Netscape Communicator's component that is used to create Web pages.

Content area: The area of the Navigator window that displays the pages of information.

Content frame: A frame that displays the contents of the selected page.

Decryption: The process of unscrambling a message using a code that matches the code used to encrypt the message.

Digital signature: Ensures that a message was actually sent by the sender, not from an impersonator.

Discussion group: A form of Internet communication that allows you to participate in interactive, ongoing discussions about a topic of common interest with people from all over the world.

Domain Name System (DNS): The e-mail addressing system used on the Internet.

Download: To copy a file to your computer from a remote site.

Eavesdrop: A security invasion in which a third party listens in on a private conversation.

E-mail: Electronic mail; a message that is sent between users on the Internet.

Emoticon: Picture of smiling or winking face used to add feeling to e-mail.

External link: A hyperlink to a file on another Web site.

Encryption: The process of scrambling a message using a code so that no one can read the message except people who have the correct decryption code.

FAQ: Documents that include answers to Frequently Asked Questions.

File Transfer Protocol (FTP): A system of rules for transferring files across the Internet.

Fixed: A font where each character takes up the same amount of space.

Fixed link: A link that identifies the file location of the destination by its full address. Also called an absolute link.

Flame: To send inflammatory remarks in an e-mail message.

Flame war: Ongoing thread of inflammatory e-mail messages.

Floating palette: A toolbar that appears in a separate window. It can be moved anywhere on the screen.

Folder: An area on your disk that is used to organize and store messages.

Followed link: A link that you have recently accessed.

Font: Set of characters with a specific design. Also called a typeface.

Form: Used to enter and submit information to a Web site.

Forward: To pass a message along to another e-mail address.

Frame: A rectangular division of the browser's display that contains a separate, scrollable page.

Frame set: A special Web page that defines the size and location of each window within the set of windows.

Freeware: Programs available on the Internet that do not require a fee for use.

Gateway: A computer that translates e-mail messages from the protocol used on one network to that used on another network.

Gopher: A menu-based interface for retrieving information stored on Gopher servers on the Internet.

GopherSpace: All the information that is available on all the Gopher servers on the Internet.

Helper application: Stand-alone program that expands the browser's capability to play sound and video file that the standard plug-ins cannot.

Hierarchy: The different categories of newsgroups.

History list: A list of locations you have accessed during your current Navigator session.

Home page: The first page of information for a Web site.

Hyperlink: *See* Hypertext link.

Hypertext link: A connection to another Web page or location on the current page.

HyperText Markup Language (HTML): The programming language used to create Web pages.

Impersonation: A security invasion in which a sender or receiver uses a false identity for communication.

Inline image: An image that loads automatically when a Web page is displayed.

Internet: A network of thousands of computer networks that allows computers to communicate with one another.

Internet Message Access Protocol (IMAP): Protocol used by the incoming mail server to deliver messages to your mailbox.

Internet Relay Chat (IRC): A program that allows simultaneous participation in a discussion over a particular Internet channel.

Internet Service Provider (ISP): A company that provides access to the Internet for a fee.

Keyword search: A method of searching by which you enter a word, words, or phrase that the search program will compare to some part of the text it has stored in the database to locate the information you are seeking.

Link: See hypertext link.

List address: E-mail address used to participate in mailing list discussions.

Listserv address: E-mail address used to subscribe to a mailing list. Also called a subscription address.

Listserver (listserv): The program used to send e-mail to and from mailing list subscribers.

Lurk: To read messages without posting to the newsgroup or mailing list.

Mail server: A computer on the Internet used for storing e-mail messages.

Mailbox: An area on the mail server that is used to store e-mail messages.

Mailer program: Program that provides the means of creating, sending, and reading e-mail messages. Also called a reader program.

Mailing list: A discussion group in which e-mail messages are sent directly to the e-mail address of every subscriber.

Manipulation: A security invasion in which a message is intercepted and changed.

Messenger: Netscape Communicator's component that is used to create, send, and store e-mail messages.

Metasearch engine: A search utility that submits your request to multiple search engines simultaneously.

Moderated: Discussion group where postings are reviewed by a moderator before being forwarded to the entire group.

Navigator: Netscape Communicator component that is used to move to and display information on the WWW.

Netiquette: The standard rules of courteous electronic communication.

Newsgroup: A discussion group in which e-mail messages are posted to the newsgroup site where they can be accessed by anyone who subscribes to the newsgroup.

Newsgroup site: A computer that participates in the Usenet network where newsgroup messages are stored.

Newsreader program: A software program used to access, read, and organize newsgroup messages.

News server: See Newsgroup site.

Nickname: A complete or shortened name used to identify a recipient of e-mail.

Plug-in: Programs that supplement the browser's capability to play sound and video. It loads automatically and runs while you are viewing the page.

Point: Unit of measurement for the height and width of characters.

Point to Point Protocol (PPP): Creates an Internet connection that checks data transfer over lines and sends it again if damaged.

Post: To send a message to a newsgroup or mailing list.

Post Office Protocol (POP): Protocol used by the incoming mail server to deliver messages to your mailbox.

Private key: The decryption code that is provided with the certificate and used to unscramble messages you receive.

Protocol: A set of rules that control how software and hardware communicate on a network.

Public key: The encryption code that is provided with the certificate and used to scramble messages you send.

Publish: The process of uploading your Web pages to a server for access by the public.

Quote: To include parts of the original e-mail message in the body of the reply.

Reader program: A program that provides the means of creating, sending, and reading e-mail messages. Also called a mailer program.

Relative link: A link based on a path in which the first part of the path is shared by both the file that contains the hyperlink and the destination file.

Rich-text document: A document that includes formatting such as bold and italics.

Router: Switches on the Internet network system that are located at network intersections and determine the best path for the packet to travel to reach its destination.

Search engine: A type of search service that typically offers no editorial content or categories.

Search service: A huge database of Internet sites that is used to locate information on the Web.

Serial Line Internet Protocol (SLIP): A set of rules similar to those for PPP, but that does not provide a damage check.

Server: A computer that holds information, providing it to clients on request.

Shareware: Programs available on the Internet that you can try before buying but which requires a fee for continued use.

Shout: To type a message in all uppercase characters.

Signature line: A personalized identification that is added to the end of the body of a message.

Simple Mail Transport Protocol (SMTP): A set of rules for sending e-mail messages over the Internet.

Smiley: Picture of smiling or winking face used to add feeling to e-mail.

Startup home page: The Web page Navigator displays when first loaded.

Stationary palette: A toolbar that is attached to a location in the window.

Store-and-forward: A system of mail forwarding that routinely holds messages for later batch sending.

Subscribe: To join a newsgroup or mailing list.

Subscription address: E-mail address used to subscribe to a mailing list. Also called a listserv address.

Tab: The bar to the left of Communicator toolbars that is used to hide and move the toolbars.

Tag: Embedded HTML code that supplies information about a Web page's structure, appearance, and contents.

Target: A marked location within a Web site to which you can create a link. Also called an anchor.

Telnet: An application that allows you to log onto and run programs on remote computers on the Internet.

Thread: A conversation in a newsgroup, with articles and responses grouped together in order.

Thumbnail: Miniature image displayed on a page that can be displayed full size by clicking on the image.

Topic search: A method of searching by navigating through a hierarchy of topic listings that group the items in a database into subject categories.

Transmission Control Protocol/Internet Protocol (TCP/IP): The core protocol used to send information on the Internet.

Troll: To deliberately post a message containing incorrect information with the intent of receiving know-it-all replies.

Typeface: Set of characters with a specific design. Also called a font.

Unfollowed link: A link that you have not recently clicked on or followed.

Uniform Resource Locator (URL): Provides location information that is used to navigate through the Internet to access a particular page.

Unmoderated: Discussion group where postings are not reviewed by a moderator before being forwarded to the entire group.

Upload: To send a file to another computer.

Usenet: The network of newsgroups on the Internet.

Variable: A font where some letters take up more space than other letters.

Wallpaper: A background image, pattern, or texture.

Web directory: A type of search service that can be searched by topic or subjects. Many include site reviews.

Web page: A document file created using HTML that is stored on a Web server and viewed using a browser.

Web site: A location on a Web server consisting of related Web pages.

White pages: An online database in which you can search for people.

World Wide Web (WWW): A part of the Internet that consists of information organized into Web pages containing text and graphic images and hypertext links.

Yellow pages: An online database in which you search for businesses.

Command
Summary

Command	Shortcut Key	Button	Action
Navigator			
File/**O**pen Page	`Ctrl` + O		Opens a page from disk
File/**S**ave As	`Ctrl` + S		Saves current document to disk
File/Save **F**rame As			Saves current frame to disk
File/Print Pre**v**iew			Displays document onscreen as it will appear when printed
File/**P**rint		[Print]	Prints current document
File/Print **F**rame			Prints current frame
File/**C**lose	`Ctrl` + W		Closes window
File/E**x**it	`Ctrl` + Q		Exits Netscape
Edit/Cu**t**	`Ctrl` + X		Cuts selected text to Clipboard
Edit/**C**opy	`Ctrl` + C		Copies selected text to Clipboard
Edit/**P**aste	`Ctrl` + V		Pastes text from Clipboard
Edit/Select **A**ll	`Ctrl` + A		Selects entire document
Edit/Pr**e**ferences/Mail & Groups/Identity			Adds a signature line to e-mail messages
Edit/Pr**e**ferences/Advanced/ Automatically load **I**mages			Turns on and off display of online image
View/Hide/Show <toolbar>			Hides or displays specified toolbar
View/**R**eload	`Ctrl` + R	[Reload]	Reloads current page
View/Page So**u**rce	`Ctrl` + U		Displays HTML code for current page
Go			Displays list of pages viewed since loading Netscape
Go/**B**ack	`Alt` + ←	[Back]	Displays last viewed page
Go/**F**orward	`Alt` + →	[Forward]	Displays next viewed page after using [Back]

Command	Shortcut Key	Button	Action
Go/**H**ome		Home	Displays startup home page
Communicator/**M**essenger Mailbox	Ctrl + 2		Opens Messenger component
Communicator/Collabra **D**iscussion Groups			Opens Collabra component
Communicator/**A**ddress Book	Ctrl + ⬆Shift + 2		Opens address book
Communicator/**B**ookmarks/ Add Bookmar**k**	Ctrl + D		Saves URL of current page
Communicator/**B**ookmarks/ Edit **B**ookmarks	Ctrl + B		Modifies location of stored bookmark
Communicator/**H**istory	Ctrl + H		Displays detailed history of pages viewed in History window
Communicator/**S**ecurity Info	Ctrl + ⬆Shift + I	Security	Displays information about a page's security settings

Booksmarks Window

Command	Shortcut Key	Button	Action
File/New **F**older			Creates a new bookmark folder
File/Go to bookmar**k**			Redisplays saved page
Edit/**D**elete	Delete		Removes bookmark from list

Messenger

Command	Shortcut Key	Button	Action
File/Empt**y** Trash Folder			Permanently deletes messages
File/Ge**t** Messages/**N**ew	Ctrl + T	Get Msg	Gets new messages from server
Edit/**U**ndo	Ctrl + Z		Reverses last action or command
Edit/**R**edo	Ctrl + Z		Repeats last action or command
Edit/Search Directory			Accesses Web directories for a person's e-mail address
View/**S**ort			Changes order of display of e-mail messages
Go/Next **U**nread Message	N	Next	Displays next unread message
Message/**N**ew Message	Ctrl + M	New Msg	Creates a new e-mail message
Message/**R**eply	Ctrl + R	Reply	Creates a reply message to sender of selected message
Message/Forwar**d**	Ctrl + L	Forward	Forwards selected message to new address

Command	Shortcut Key	Button	Action
Collabra			
File/Su**b**scribe to Discussion Groups		[Subscribe]	Subscribes to selected newsgroup
Edit/**D**elete Discussion Group			Removes subscribed newsgroup
Edit/Cancel Mess**a**ge	Delete		Deletes posted message
Message/**R**eply/to **G**roup	Ctrl + D	[Reply]	Creates a reply message to newsgroup
Composition Window			
File/Send **L**ater			Stores e-mail to be sent at a later time
F**o**rmat/**S**tyle/**B**old	Ctrl + B	**A**	Bolds selected text
F**o**rmat/**S**tyle/**I**talics	Ctrl + I	*A*	Italicizes selected text
Tools/Check **S**pelling		[Spelling]	Starts the Spell-Checker feature
Composer			
File/P**u**blish		[Publish]	Uploads current file to a server
File/**B**rowse Page		[Preview]	Displays page in browser window
View/Page So**u**rce	Ctrl + U		Displays HTML code for current page
Insert/**L**ink	Ctrl + ⇧Shift + L	[Link]	Creates a hypertext link
Insert/T**a**rget		[Target]	Creates an anchor
Insert/**I**mage		[Image]	Adds an image to a page
Insert/**H**orizontal Line		[H. Line]	Inserts horizontal line across page
F**o**rmat/**C**olor		[▪▼]	Changes text color
F**o**rmat/**H**eading		[Normal ▼]	Applies predefined paragraph style
F**o**rmat/**L**ist/**B**ulletted		[≔]	Creates bulletted list of selected text
F**o**rmat/**A**lign		[≣▼]	Changes position of lines between margins
F**o**rmat/Pa**g**e Colors and Properties			Changes color of text and background

Index

Notes